HOW TO INTERPRET
YOUR DREAMS

Practical Techniques
Based on the
Edgar Cayce Readings

Mark A. Thurston, Ph.D.

ARE
PRESS
ASSOCIATION FO
RESEARCH AN
ENLIGHTENMEN1

A.R.E. PRESS • VIRGINIA BEACH • VIRGINIA

ACKNOWLEDGEMENTS

I would like to thank many people who have been very helpful to me in the completion of this book. Typing of the text from my longhand notes was done by Anna Holman, Claire Grant and Judy FitzGerald. The critical job of good editing was done by Bob Smith and Ken Skidmore. (I even had dreams of Bob editing specific chapters before I could get them written in the waking state!)

And my appreciation is also extended to friends and colleagues who have shared ideas and inspired me with their visions of dreaming—especially, Herbert Puryear, Harmon Bro, Scott Sparrow, Marilyn Peterson and Henry Reed.

And finally I want to thank those members of *A Search for God* Study Groups who helped me by submitting some of their own dreams. Although only a few of the dreams appear directly in the text of the book as examples, sharing all those dreams with me was an important part of the creation of this book.

CONTENTS

Introduction

The title of this book promises quite a bit. However, after considering dozens of other alternatives, I was left with the conclusion that the title should say as simply as possible just what I hoped to accomplish in writing this book. I want you, the reader, to have a sense of confidence that you can take that sometimes bizarre experience we call a dream and make some sense of it.

This book has two purposes: first, it is an effort to explain a theory and a philosophy of dreams and dreaming. In the long run, it is probably not to our advantage to jump immediately into techniques without a clear understanding of the assumptions and background on which they are based. The primary source materials that I have used in developing the theoretical framework are the psychic readings of Edgar Cayce. In the hundreds of dreams he interpreted from a self-induced altered state of consciousness, there emerges a sophisticated understanding of why and how we dream.

A second purpose of the book is to develop applicable tools and techniques which you can use to interpret your own dreams. Many of these have been drawn from Cayce's interpretations; others have come from various dream theories or from my own experience. When you finish this book I hope you will have acquired specific skills that you can use to understand better and to apply your dreams.

The Edgar Cayce readings, as well as many other sources, clearly indicate that this topic of dreams is worthy of our careful consideration. The following statement from the readings came in 1923; it holds true for me today.

In this age, at present, 1923, there is not sufficient credence given dreams; for the best development of the human family is to give the greater increase in knowledge of the subconscious, soul or spirit world. This is a *dream.*   3744-4

This principle is beautifully illustrated in a dream brought to Edgar Cayce for interpretation (900-243, Q-3). In the dream experience the man was crossing an avenue, asleep and yet conscious. That is, he was aware of the trolley cars and vehicles that were endangering him. All around him things were dreary and rainy, and he felt his way about, unable to awaken to his surroundings. Finally a policeman guided him to safety and the dreamer simply rested on him, relying and trusting in him fully. Cayce's interpretation of this dream states that it demonstrates that the dreamer is "awakening to the possibilities of the use of the unseen forces." These influences from within the subconscious mind can be relied upon for guidance and direction. Especially through the study of his dreams which come from the subconscious mind, this dreamer and each of us can expect to find a reliable source of understanding and direction.

In many ways most books are autobiographical. I can say, without reservation, that dreams have been a potent source of guidance and direction in my life. What I hope to share with you, the reader, in this book is a chronicle of my emerging understanding of the adventure of dreams and their application.

This book may not appear to be autobiographical because there is not a chronological development. However, my life, like yours, grows in ways other than through time. There are patterns perhaps far more important than the orderly flow of days and years. There is a pattern of meaning that reveals itself to us in its own time and in its own way.

This special pattern is one which leads to fulfillment in life—not only higher states of awareness but also a rich and joyful appreciation of life, oneself and others. It is a progression or an unfoldment that was suggested in the psychic readings of Edgar Cayce as *A Search for God.* In essence it is a step-by-step development of qualities of consciousness: cooperation, self-knowledge, ideals, etc. We can expect that it is relevant to the wide range of endeavors, including small group dynamics, personal growth, building institutions, and even dream study.

Although there are twenty-four lessons or steps in the *A Search for God* sequence, it has seemed to me that some of them are more directly relevant to dream study than are others. And so, I have selected about half of the two dozen progressive steps and formulated a developmental approach to working (and playing!) with your dreams. The reader who has already studied the *A Search for God* material will quickly recognize the respective lessons by glancing at the table of contents of this book.

Since the *A Search for God* readings of Cayce have most frequently been used in the small group format (i.e., a nationwide Study Group program), the question will naturally arise as to whether or not a purpose of this book is to start dream study groups. The answer is no. It is my hope that many of you will work with the concepts in this book through an involvement in a Search for God small group. In fact, you will notice that many of the exercises at the ends of chapters suggest this kind of format. However, it has *not* been my intention to start a new and separate study group program which concerns itself merely with dreams. The reason for this lies right at the heart of the approach to dream interpretation you will find in this book. Stated briefly, it says: we can never work only on a dream; we must concern ourselves with the dream *and* the dreamer.

Another way of expressing this fundamental element of my approach is that we cannot have a mere technology of dream interpretation. For example, I doubt that we could ever build a computer system to interpret a dream in the fullest sense of what that should mean. Not only must we include the individual associations the dreamer might have with the dream symbols, but more importantly we must appreciate that there is an on-going element in most every dream. The dream does not end when we wake up and write it down. It is an illustration of something going on within us and to work on interpreting a dream also means a willingness to work on ourselves, the dreamers.

A way in which we work on ourselves is to get involved in some type of regular effort at self-understanding and spiritual growth. There are many approaches to do this; one excellent method in my own opinion is to join a Study Group that includes prayer and meditation as part of its consistent disipline. The *A Search for God* Study Group program sponsored by the Association for Research and Enlightenment is a good example of this. Groups such as this may choose to work with dreams as part of their weekly meeting, perhaps using a book such as this one as a resource. However, in my opinion, it is important that the group refrain from becoming simply a dream discussion group. Including the prayer and meditation is particularly important if group members are to deal most effectively with the dreams *and* themselves as dreamers. Most likely a portion of each meeting devoted to the

A Search for God textbook itself will provide a helpful "balance" to the study of dreams.

For those of you unable to join a Study Group, the same principle holds true. As you work with the skills and techniques of this book, be sure also to include regular periods of study, prayer and meditation. It is just this combination— appreciation for the dream and the dreamer—which can make working with one's dreams an adventure well worth the taking.

Chapter One
THE LEVELS OF MIND: HOW DO DREAMS HAPPEN?

In order to unravel the mystery of our dreams, we should begin by exploring the nature of the mind itself. Although we might prefer a more direct beginning—such as a consideration of the meaning of particular symbols—a truly comprehensive and practical approach to dream interpretation requires a foundation. That foundation is an understanding of the levels of mind and how they interact with each other to produce a dream. In other words, to be able to interpret a particular dream accurately, we must have a basic notion of what went into that dream's creation. This principle makes sense for solving any mystery. For example, if we were given a difficult knot to untie, a series of illustrations depicting how the knot was formed would undoubtedly be helpful to us.

We can all relate to the fact that the mind is made up of more than one level or aspect. As an illustration, nearly everyone has had the experience of trying to remember some fact (such as a person's name) that he "knows" quite well but simply cannot recall at that moment. Undoubtedly that information is within the mind; yet, at least temporarily, it is not accessible to what we can call the "conscious mind." Rather, the elusive fact is a part of an unconscious layer of mind. This is our first fundamental principle for understanding how a dream is created: A very real (and, we might add, "very extensive") aspect of our mind exists outside our conscious awareness. Although this may seem to be quite an elementary assumption, we should appreciate the fact that only in the past one hundred years or so has such a notion been commonly accepted.

Mind Is the Builder

Before looking more closely at what levels of mind may exist within this vast region we have called the unconscious, it would be well to consider an important concept from the Cayce readings about the creative function of mind. This concept

1

relates the activities of the mind to the two other principal aspects of our being—the physcial and the spiritual. It is expressed as a formula which says, "The spirit is the life, mind is the builder, and the physical is the result." The first portion of this triune formula is simply a restatement of the Cayce concept that there is only one fundamental energy or force in the universe and it is a spiritual life force. The second phrase suggests that whenever that spiritual life force expresses itself, it does so in terms of a pattern or a form; the mind is what gives that essential force or energy its pattern of expression. In other words, the mind is the creative (or building) function within us. The final portion of the formula says that what we experience in the physical or material realm of life is the result of what we have created or built mentally.

Certainly not everything we think of takes on physical form, but this does not mean that our unmanifested thoughts lack reality. Rather, with every thought we have created something, using the spiritual life force. Thoughts are things (or thought forms), even the ones that never seem to manifest in our material world. We shall see later that thought creation takes place at another dimension of reality (or, to use a phrase more easily understood, at another vibratory level of energy). For the time being, suffice it to say that our thoughts are very real—so real, in fact, that we often meet our own thought forms as the images of our dreams.

Analogies of the Mind

The triune formula just outlined suggests that the mind is essentially creative in nature. And yet we have probably all experienced times when our mental activity didn't seem very creative; instead, it may have seemed very habitual or reactive in nature. This experience points out a dual quality of mind—it is both the creative principle within us and the storehouse of our habitual patterns of thinking, feeling and acting. Several analogies can help clarify these roles.

A film projector. This analogy was proposed in a question in a reading (900-156) and received Edgar Cayce's approval. Although the original analogy involved a movie projector, a modern slide projector is probably more accurate. In this case, the bulb of the projector corresponds to the spiritual life force; the individual slides are the habitual ways of thinking or feeling that have been built over time; and the image projected onto the screen corresponds to the physical results or our actions in the world. As depicted in the illustration below, there is a wide variety of slides available to be projected—that is, mental patterns ranging from resentment and selfishness to love and healing. These thought-form patterns are stored within the individual's own unconscious mind and may be confronted in dreams. It can be a matter of personal choice or merely one of habit as to which patterns (or slides) are projected into expression in our physical lives.

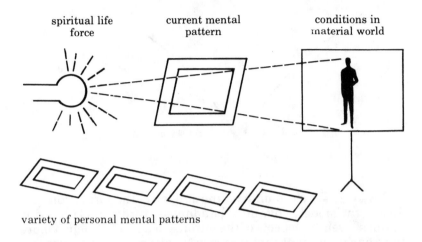

spiritual life force   current mental pattern   conditions in material world

variety of personal mental patterns

A tape recorder. The concept of a stored pattern of thinking or feeling can also be represented by the analogy of a tape recording. This analogy is especially significant in pointing out that a pattern is not erased simply by replaying it. If that were the case, we could play a tape recorded message or song only once. Similarly, a painful or traumatic memory is not healed by *merely* recalling it. What is required is a replacement. In our dreams we frequently encounter memory patterns in the unconscious mind that require such a "healing by replacement" process.

A player piano. This device is an especially good analogue to the mind, because it illustrates its dual nature. Just as the player piano can use a roll to repeat with little effort the same tune time and again, we can fall into habitual patterns of mental activity (i.e., saying, thinking, feeling the same old thing in a recurrent situation). However, it is also possible to turn off the roller of the player piano, sit down at the keyboard, and create a new tune. In the same way, we always have the choice of mentally building or creating a new thought pattern, rather than being controlled by an old one. Many of our dreams point out such opportunities to us.

Levels of the Unconscious Mind

When compared to the contents of the unconscious, the conscious mind is like the tip of an iceberg. If we invert the iceberg in this analogy, we get a model like the one developed by Dr. Herbert Puryear* based on one of Edgar Cayce's dreams (294-131).

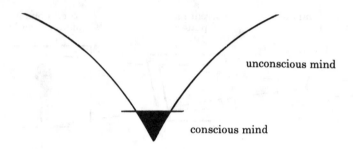

unconscious mind

conscious mind

However, for us to understand properly the formation of a dream, the model above must be adapted in order to: (1) describe various levels or aspects of the unconscious, and (2) depict more than one individual's mind (for we shall see that some dreams involve telepathic communication). The Swiss psychiatrist C.G. Jung proposed a two-level unconscious consisting of the personal unconscious mind (a storehouse of personal memories) and, beyond that, a collective unconscious (the storehouse of mental patterns that are inherent to all human beings). Like Jung's theory, the Edgar Cayce readings describe a *subconscious mind,* which includes the personal unconscious, as described by Jung, plus a variety of levels beyond that, which are characterized as "universal." In this case "universal" does not mean "omniscient," but "accessible to all persons." Various terms have been used to label these layers of mind, among them being the astral plane, the etheric plane, etc.

Beyond the subconscious mind is the *superconscious mind,* which is the Divine Mind within us all. When we make our awareness one with this level of mind we experience our oneness with God, our oneness with all life, and the eternalness of our soul. Although dreams in which the superconscious mind is experienced directly are very rare, the Cayce readings suggest that we will find the influence of this highest level of mind expressing frequently in our dreams.

Finally, it should be noted that the use of the word "beyond" to characterize these levels of mind (e.g., "the superconscious

*See *Meditation and the Mind of Man,* by Herbert Puryear and Mark Thurston, available from A.R.E. Press, Virginia Beach, Va.

lies *beyond* the subconscious") is meant to imply not spatial location of parts of the mind, but the way that we come to experience them. The habitual memory patterns of the subconscious act as a barrier to our contact with the superconscious. It is only by dealing with those subconscious mental patterns that a consistent contact can be maintained with the superconscious mind. We shall see that dream study and meditation are two of the most effective ways to deal with those subconscious thought-form patterns.

We can now redraw our model to depict the concepts just described.

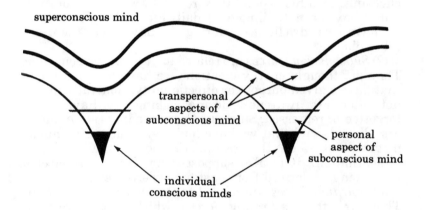

Types of Forces Producing Dreams

The various levels of mind have an effect on our lives in the physical world through what the Cayce readings call "patterning forces." In other words, our thought-form creations are very real and *exert an influence on our lives.* This influence is so real and direct that one reading states "thought becomes as material in the subconscious. . .as a physical act in the material world." (900-65) "Patterning" is an especially descriptive word, because our memories shape or mold our physical experience. The term "forces" implies that these thought forms are not just expressions of energy, but energy that has a *direction.* (Think about the types of force you experience in daily life—such as gravitational force or the force you use to open a door—and you will see that there is always a direction associated with them.) And so, a patterning force is not only something that is influencing us, it is also something

5

that is leading us somewhere in our own growth in consciousness. Some directions are probably more desirable than others, but a consideration of that will have to wait for the chapter concerning ideals in our dreams.

In summary, the levels of mind—conscious, subconscious and superconscious—directly influence our physical lives through patterning forces. It is this notion of forces that the Cayce readings rely on in defining how a dream happens. We shall encounter the following terms frequently in the relevant readings:

(1) *Mental forces* are related to the conscious mind. They can be thought of as those patterning forces that we are entertaining in conscious awareness or that we are recurrently choosing. In other words, they relate to what our conscious minds have been dwelling on in daily life (and especially what we have been dwelling on during the day before the dream takes place).

(2) *Subconscious forces* are related to the subconscious mind. They are thought-energy creations we have personally built that have a given purpose or directionality. Generally they do not enter into awareness during waking life, having been forgotten or repressed. Since the Cayce readings state that we are all souls and that we have had many successive human incarnations (i.e., the readings espouse the theory of reincarnation), it is also supposed that some subconscious forces may be derived from past life experiences.

(3) *Spiritual forces* are related to the superconscious mind. They are the patterning forces which result from the consciousness of wholeness and oneness characteristic of the superconscious mind. Such a pattern has not been created by us; it is, rather, something that has been "given" and exists within the mind of each soul—that image of perfection in which we were created (see Genesis 1:27). For the most part, this pattern exists primarily as a potentiality within us, and the spiritual forces are an influence or impetus toward the realization of that potential. They show up in our dreams especially as direct guidance or warnings.

Dreams as the Forces in Interaction

We have now developed a sufficient number of concepts to begin examining the various descriptions in the Cayce readings of how a dream happens. First is the idea that a dream can be a type of reasoning. This may initially seem incongruent with our experience, because dreams frequently seem very unreasonable, even nonsensical. However, the reasoning which produces a dream is *inductive reasoning* and is performed by the subconscious. This is in contrast to *deductive reasoning,* which is most frequently employed by the conscious mind. The difference between the two is actually quite simple and straightforward. In reasoning inductively we take a series of specific facts or observations and arrive at a general principle (e.g., this winter I have observed on twenty occasions a brown-tailed rabbit whose fur has turned white; and so, I reason that this species of animal changes fur coloring each winter). With deductive reasoning we take a given general principle or assumption and infer specific conclusions from it (e.g., I assume that all horses have four legs, so when you tell me you are bringing your horse in to be shod, I get four horseshoes ready before you arrive).

By distinguishing these two types of reasoning we obtain a clue to help us understand this first definition of dreams from the readings: ". . .that as seen [in dreams] is the force of the subconscious with inductive reasoning." (294-38) In other words, a dream can be produced by a reasoning activity of the subconscious mind in which it *seeks to discover an underlying principle* behind a series of specific memories and experiences that may seem unrelated. Here may be at least a part of the reason why our dreams so often seem to be a jumble of characters, places and actions. There is a type of reasoning going on (although a type unlike the one our conscious, rational minds most frequently use) which seeks to find a unifying principle or concept behind the fragments of our waking experiences.

However, this first definition fails to include an important activity which also can produce a dream: the *interaction* of the spiritual, subconscious and mental forces. Two types of interaction are described in other readings. First is the *correlation* of subconscious forces with mental forces. Those who have taken statistics will recall that a correlational analysis is one in which we seek to determine whether or not there is a meaningful relationship between two sets of data (i.e., between two sets of experiences). Of special note is that in doing a correlation we are *not* concerned with whether or not one set of experiences *caused* another set of experiences; rather, we ask if the two are *related in a meaningful way.* This explanation of how a dream happens suggests that there is an interaction of subconscious forces (recall that these are related to our subconscious memory patterns) with mental forces (related to our conscious, waking experiences), and this interaction is for the purpose of discovering a meaningful relationship between the two. A simple example of this would be a dream which shows us that perhaps the angry thoughts experienced yesterday (mental forces) are related to a forgotten childhood experience that was never resolved (subconscious forces). The following passage from the readings describes this type of process.

[In dreams] there is given the correlation of the mental mind [i.e., the mental forces] with the subconscious forces of the entity, and as the conscious mind only reasons by comparison, and the subconscious by inductive reasoning, then the correlation of these are presented in the manner that is often emblematical. . .   137-60

Without our previous discussion of terminology, this passage would probably seem quite enigmatic. We can note that it refers not only to correlation, but also to the different methods of reasoning.

Correlations that produce dreams do not have to be limited to an interaction of subconscious and mental forces. Four distinct factors can be involved in such correlational interactions: the condition of the physical body, mental forces, subconscious forces and spiritual forces. We might add that any or all of these factors *in another person* might also be involved in a correlation that produces a dream (e.g., correlation of one person's subconscious forces with the subconscious forces of another, producing a telepathic dream).

A second type of interaction which can be involved in the production of a dream is *projection*. The process to which the readings are referring in using this term is not the type of psychological projection in which one's own qualities are imagined to be those of others. Instead, it is much like the projection of a slide or movie onto a screen. A projection results when something casts an image, a direct representation of itself, onto a surface. That "something" can be a mental force that projects its image or pattern onto the "surface" of the subconscious forces. This may not sound much different from a correlation between the two, but it is different and it may produce a distinct quality of dream experience, depending on what is being projected. The difference here may be compared to the one between a boss coming into the office and *announcing* how things are going to be done (i.e., a direct projection of his idea onto the "surface" of the employee's thinking and acting) and a boss sitting down and *discussing* with his employee how things are going to be done (i.e., looking for meaningful relationships between their ideas). In the following two instances the readings suggest that the particular dream being interpreted is primarily the product of the mental forces (i.e., what has been consciously thought during the day) forcing their impressions onto the dream.

. . .these are of the entity's own making, visioning through that of the attempt, as it were, (unconscious it may have been) to force issues, as conditions are arising in the mental and physical forces of the entity.   900-261

In the various dreams as come to the body from time to time, these may be inundations of the mental consciousness of the body, so—as has been oft given—do not force the issue too often with self.   900-348

The possibility of dreams being produced by such projections shall have to be considered in the approaches we use to interpret a dream.

Further Dream Definitions

We have looked at some relatively technical definitions of dreams—concerning inductive reasoning, projection and correlation—and we should consider as well some of the *functional* definitions from the readings. This amounts to defining dreams in terms of what they do or what they provide for us.

In these functional definitions we will frequently encounter the word "vision," which is used in a manner that is somewhat different from how it is usually understood. Rather than referring to a somewhat mystical appearance (e.g., visions of transcendent reality), the term "vision" is used to describe a dreamlike experience in which the spiritual forces, ideals and attitudes impart an influence. In contrast to this, the term "dream" denotes an experience which relates primarily to physical health or the physical body. This distinction is explained in the following passage.

Q-5. [379]: Are my dreams ever significant of spiritual awakening?
A-5. As is experienced by the entity, there are dreams and visions and experiences. When only dreams, these *too* are significant—but rather of that of the physical health, or physical conditions. In visions there is oft the *inter-between* giving expressions that make for an awakening between the mental consciousness, or that that has been turned over and over in the physical consciousness and mind being weighed with that the self holds as its ideal.   262-9

It is hoped that the preceding discussion will be helpful for purposes of understanding the verbatim excerpts from the Cayce readings which will be used. However, no attempt will be made in the text of this book itself to distinguish between "dreams" and "visions."

At least six functional definitions of dreams can be found in the readings. Among them are the following.

A dream is an actual experience or activity of the soul. Many people have the tendency to think of a dream as a type of meaningless fantasy; however, the readings suggest that to some extent a dream experience is more "real" than a waking one. Of course we must be careful in using the word "real." In this instance it simply means that a dream experience may encompass a truer perspective of the nature of mind, energy and human relations than the perspective we have when we are awake. In this regard we might say that when we are "awake" we are actually "asleep" to the sense of being an infinite soul. In one reading we find the statement, ". . .for such experiences as dreams, visions or the like, are but the *activities in the unseen world* of the real self of an entity." (5754-3) The phrase "unseen world" is not intended to mystify us. It simply refers to dimensions of reality or levels of vibration which are different from our everyday, material world. Actually these "unseen worlds" of experience can be much like our material world, only seemingly vaster because with a thought, our awareness can "travel." In the words of one reading, "There is no difference in the unseen world to that that is visible, save in the unseen so much greater expanse or space may be covered." (5754-3)

The dream events and symbols we recall are rarely the actual experiences or activities of the soul. The experience itself is usually symbolically depicted in terms of mental or physical events from the past (i.e., the available "vocabulary of memories" with which our dream world speaks to our conscious recall). This process of translating a soul experience into symbolic or emblematic dream form is described in the following reading:

The experience for the mind of the soul. . .is often tempered by the physical or mental experiences of the body, and when such is the case these then are presented often in emblematical ways and manners. 302-3

As a final note on this first functional definition of a dream, we should not suppose that every experience of the soul in dreams is Truth. In other words, the scope of a dream experience may include a broader perspective of reality, but this does not entail infallibility. For example, imagine that in waking life a man meets a woman and becomes very friendly with her. He gives her considerable attention and spends much time listening to her concerns and offering to help where he can. In this case, imagine that his attraction to her is primarily a physical one, and that his actions are primarily motivated by the hope of getting on her good side. He refuses to admit to himself this sexual attraction and rationalizes that he is doing all this for altruistic reasons. Then he begins to have frequent dreams of a love affair with this woman. Certainly, under different circumstances the dreams might have a different meaning; but in this case, they probably depict his real motivation in the relationship. In other words, the dreams are experiences of his soul in which there is a confrontation with his desire and motivation, and they give a more realistic picture of his motives than the one he consciously claims to have. However, these dreams do not necessarily represent a great Truth—that is, they are not necessarily encouraging a sexual relationship with the woman.

A dream usually is a description of the conditions that exist in or among the levels of our being. Sometimes we want a dream to be more than just a statement of the current conditions. We may prefer to say, "The dream told me to do such-and-such." However, the fact of the matter is that for most dreamers it is infrequent that a dream makes the choice. It is left to us to infer what ought to be done and to use the will to do it. The value of a dream which simply depicts the existing conditions is that it may do so from a better (or at least different) perspective than our conscious one. This function of a dream is clearly stated in the readings in the following manner:

"In dreams, visions and experiences, each individual soul passes through or reviews or sees from a different attitude those experiences of its own activities." 257-136

As an analogy, imagine standing so that you face a column of individuals. From this perspective you may be able to see the first person in the column quite clearly, but you see the rest of the people only partially, if at all. However, if you move to a new perspective (several yards to either side) you may be able to see the same conditions in a far more informative way. An aerial view of your different perspectives would look like this:

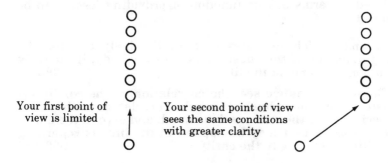

Your first point of view is limited

Your second point of view sees the same conditions with greater clarity

In this analogy, the people in the columns, of course, represent the various conditions (mental and physical) which affect our lives.

A dream can give an insight into God's law or His working in our lives. This is simply stated in the readings: "Through this manner [in a dream] the entity gains the insight to the spiritual forces manifesting in the material world." (900-144) That insight can come as understanding. In our personal spiritual search we may at times feel as if we are making all the effort to reach towards the Infinite and wonder if the Infinite is reaching towards us in a supportive, helpful way. Despite such doubts, God does take an initiative in our development, and a primary activity of this nature is manifested in our dreams. Through them God or the spiritual forces can have a direct association with us—an association which has understanding as its purpose.

[Dreams are a] *natural* experience! It's *not* an unnatural! Don't seek for unnatural or supernatural! It is natural—it is nature—it is God's activity! His associations with man, His *desire* to make for man a way for an understanding! 5754-3

Yes, we have the body-mind here, with those dreams as come to the entity, and through which the entity may gain the more perfect understanding of the relations between God and man, and the way in which He, God, manifests himself through mankind. 900-143

A dream can present a lesson to be applied. There is an instructive function active in dreams. Of course, the great lesson to be learned is the reality and responsibility of our divine nature—our oneness with God. The quality and effectiveness of our dream instruction is dependent on many factors; among them are our ideals, the degree of attunement of our body and mind with those ideals, and the extent of our efforts to apply or put into practice the dream lessons of previous nights. In the following two passages, dreams are defined in terms of this function of providing lessons to be applied.

Dreams which are presented to the body are for the enlightenment of the consciousness of the body, if the body would apply same in the life. 3937-1

The dreams, as we see, the correlation of the conditions existent in the physical mind, correlated with those experiences of the subconscious mind, and give to the entity those lessons that may be applied in the life, as regarding conditions relating to the entity. 900-185

A dream can provide a solution to a problem. This is one of the most immediately applicable functions through which a dream can help us. The problem can be very abstract (such as how to solve a difficult math equation) or very concrete (such as where to find some old photographs that have been misplaced).

We have probably all heard stories of great inventions or creative ideas that have come through dreams. Elias Howe is said to have had an insight-giving dream which showed him where to place the thread in the needle, leading to the invention of the sewing machine. F.A. Kekule, the discoverer of the benzene ring in chemistry, is said to have dreamed of a snake swallowing its own tail, which led him to an understanding of molecular structure that had eluded him. Great authors, such as Robert Louis Stevenson, have used dreams to answer the problem of what they should write next.

Apparently, the key to making use of this potential function of a dream is to go to sleep with a clearly defined question or problem in mind. Furthermore, it should be a problem on which you have made considerable conscious effort to reach a solution. This problem-solving function is mentioned in the following dream definition. (Recall that "mental forces" refers to mental patterns that have recently been held consciously in waking life.)

Now, the dreams as we see come to the entity are in the way and manner as have been outlined as these do present themselves...in visions from the body-conscious mind seeking solutions of conditions in the mental forces of the body...
900-231

A dream can be an attunement to likely future circumstances. This function of a dream will be explored in greater depth in a later section on precognition in dreams. The notion that, *with great regularity,* our dreams give a preview of future events is rather unique to the dream theory of the Cayce readings. Such a dream function is mentioned in the following two passages. In the second passage, the term "advance of the consciousness" is used to describe this process.

Hence as thought and purpose and aim and desire are set in motion by minds, their effect is as a condition that *is...Dream* is but *attuning* an individual mind to those individual storehouses of experience that has been set in motion. Hence at times there may be the perfect connection, at others there may be the static of interference...
262-83

In this [dream] we find still the advance of the consciousness as in awakening in the individual forces of the entity...
900-97

The first passage contains most of the significant concepts for understanding how this particular dream function takes place. By such mental activity as our thoughts and desires we create thought forms that are very real. These thought forms are stored within us; and as they express themselves in our physical lives, they are influencing or even determining our future experiences. In other words, we are creating our future physical experiences right now by the kind of thought forms we are building.

Since a dream is created in the realm of our thought forms, it is a preview of what probably lies ahead. We must use the word "probably" because a dream does not tune in to a future that is fixed. One can always use the will to alter what has been set in motion by previous thoughts and desires. A precognitive dream simply says, "Here is what is going to occur according to the patterns that have been established and set in motion." We should also note the modifying sentence at the end of the first passage. Not every dream is a prediction of future events. A precognitive dream will occur only as we attune ourselves to such forces within the mind and to the degree that we desire and need such advance warning.

Categories of Dreams

The meaning of dreams can be so elusive that many theorists have tried to categorize them as a first step in interpretation. An example of this would be the attempt to define a particular dream as physical, mental, emotional or spiritual. This may or may not be the most fruitful way to classify dream experiences; however, it is a step in the right direction because it shows an appreciation for the fact that the mind can produce a variety of types of dream experiences.

We have already examined one categorical breakdown of dream experiences in the Cayce readings: the difference between a "dream" and a "vision." More frequently, the readings describe a three-part division of dream experiences. Unfortunately, at first glance there appear to be several three-part divisions suggested in various readings. This can be frustrating, because we read one reading and find a careful, clear distinction between three types of dream experience, then we find another reading that seems to suggest a different three-part division. However, with careful study we find that there is some common ground among these various categorical breakdowns. In fact, what at first appears to be a collection of many different classification systems, which confuses the issue, turns out to be a series of variations on a single formulation that defines three basic types of dream experience.

In simplest terms, the three categories of dreams are produced by: (1) physical conditions, (2) elements of the personality, and (3) elements beyond the personality (i.e., the mind of the soul). Looking more clearly at each of these types of dreams, we have:

1. Physically produced dreams simply reflect conditions in the body, and especially conditions related to imbalances in assimilation (i.e., the digestive system). Nightmares are of this variety; and any time we have an especially jumbled or frightening dream we should begin our work with the dream by asking ourselves, "Was my body (particularly my digestive system) out of balance last night?" Apparently, when our bodies are not able to digest and assimilate food properly it produces a stress on the imaginative forces of the mind, giving rise to bizarre dreams. Some of the readings which mention this first basic category of dream are as follows:

There are those [dreams] that are of the purely physical nature—the reaction of properties taken in the system when digestion is not in keeping with assimilations, and then one experiences those conditions that may be called nightmares.
4167-1

Because the activities of this particular system allow the poor assimilations. . .these act upon the bodily forces themselves so as to make for the harrowing experiences at times.
Hence we have what in the reaction is the activity of the principles of the foods, or that taken for such activity acts upon the imaginative forces. . .
1472-2

First these are dreams that are produced by conditions of the digestive system of a physical body.
900-13

2. Elements of the conscious personality are, in effect, the mental forces of an individual. In this second category of dreams our concerns of the day are being weighed. Sometimes a dream of this nature will produce a solution; at other times, just a depiction of our worries, desires, etc. Since this is the category of dream that especially relates to elements of the personality, it can include the dreams in which we pick up on personal conditions (mental or physical) of *another* person—telepathic dreams. This type of dream is mentioned in the second selection from the readings defining this category.

Then there is the mental condition of the body wherein worry, trouble, or any unusual action of the mind—mentally—physically—causes seeking for the way and manner of understanding. This may bring either the action of the subconscious with the mental abilities of the body, or it may bring wholly correlations of material sensuous conditions. These may appear in the form of visions that are in a manner the key to the situations, or they may appear in conditions as warnings, taking on conditions that are as illustrations or experiences.   4167-1

Then there are those [dream] manifestations that come as the correlation of mental forces in a physical body to the mental forces of other bodies and conditions.   900-13

3. The mind of the soul can produce dreams which introduce an understanding or awareness beyond that which we have had through the waking personality. Dreams of this kind produce a sense of discovery and the unveiling of a truth or lesson. The forces active in this category are primarily the subconscious and spiritual forces.

Then there is the action of the purely subconscious forces, giving lessons to the body out of its own experiences. 4167-1

Then the third character: those visions or experiences of the superconscious or soul-self.   1472-2

Then there are the relations of the mental with those of the spiritual conditions of an entity, from which the mental of a living physical entity may gain impressions.   900-13

Except in the case of nightmares or bizarre dreams, it does not seem that Cayce's theory of three dream categories is particularly helpful for dream interpretation. However, this concept makes at least two significant contributions to our dream work. The first is that it helps us realize that *no one interpretation approach will work on every dream,* simply because there exists a variety of internal mechanisms or processes which produce dreams. The second is that it shows us that not every dream is necessarily divine guidance or a message from the soul. We must learn to walk that narrow line between dismissing dreams as fantasy on the one side and ascribing a quality of infallibility to them on the other.

Meditation and the Levels of the Mind

The topic of meditation is pertinent to nearly every chapter of this book. The same forces and energy patterns that produce dreams are operative in meditation. The reader is strongly encouraged to keep a consistent daily meditation period as part of the study of this book or as part of any attempt to work with dreams. For those not familiar with the approach to meditation described in the Edgar Cayce readings, a brief instructional guide is provided in Appendix A. For a more thorough discussion, the reader may wish to consult *Meditation and the Mind of Man.**

In meditation, through our focus of attention upon the single thought of our spiritual ideal we are reprogramming our habitual mental patterns and desires. We are transforming the way in which the spiritual, subconscious and mental forces will interact with each other. It should be no surprise that meditation will change the quality of our dreams. If we meditate we are moving toward better attunement, and hence we are likely to have dreams that (1) show less "interference of conscious forces" (853-8), (2) contain fewer "distressing" elements (1472-2), and (3) present more "profound" insights and messages (900-240).

And entering into meditation. . .one then submerges the physical consciousness and allows an attunement. . .

As has been given for this entity, such an attunement or such an awareness becomes most in accord in dream; for then there is the submerging of the physical consciousness and the desires of same; and if there is the meditating it brings better attunement with less of what may be termed as an interference of conscious forces, conscious influences.   853-8

Q-4. How can I become rid of the following conditions: First, distressing dreams?

A-4. By attuning each portion of the system to a oneness of energy. By the meditation and coordination of the activities in the system.   1472-2

. . .as the consciousness of the *entity* becomes nearer to that one consciousness—that is, as the body-conscious, the physical or sensuous consciousness, and the subconscious-ness, becomes nearer in one, or nearer in accord with each, the visions, the dreams, as are seen, are more profound in their presentation.   900-240

Summary

As ordinary as is the dream, it is still our most accessible window inward to the soul. This commonplace, nightly experience is a regular view of the extraordinary world of the

---

*Meditation and the Mind of Man, by Herbert Puryear and Mark Thurston, available from A.R.E. Press, Box 595, Virginia Beach, VA 23451.

unconscious mind. As soon as we begin to turn our attention to dreams, we are impressed by the variety of experiences they can provide. In fact, that variety can be almost overwhelming when we start trying to unlock the meanings of our dreams. Without a roadmap of the unconscious, we will quickly become confused or frustrated in working with our dreams.

The first step in our attempt to secure such a roadmap has been to examine the mind itself—its capabilities and functions, as well as its levels or divisions. Directly related to the levels of mind are the forces which produce dreams: spiritual, subconscious and mental forces. Through inductive reasoning and the interaction of forces a dream is produced.

However, an effective roadmap must tell us more than just how the mind produces a dream. Our efforts at interpretation are likely to fail unless we know what purposes or functions a dream potentially fulfills. The Cayce readings include six such functional definitions of dreams. The readings further point out three primary categories of dream experience, each requiring a distinct approach for interpretation. Before turning to specific interpretation techniques, however, we will examine methods of developing a cooperative relationship with our dream world. This is the topic of the next chapter, which will complete the foundation for our understanding of Edgar Cayce's approach to interpreting dreams.

Chapter Two
COOPERATING WITH THE UNCONSCIOUS MIND

When we think about our own unconscious minds, what qualities occur to us? There may be a tendency to imagine the unconscious to be of a threatening or confusing nature. The Freudian notion of repressed sexual content may suggest to us that we would be better off not to explore the unconscious; films such as *The Exorcist* imply the possibility of an overwhelming demonic nature. Thus, in order to develop a cooperative, friendly relationship with the unseen side of ourselves we may need to overcome some cultural prejudices.

One way to begin this process is to examine the dreams of individuals who have found that their unconscious minds apparently really want to help—that the unconscious frequently tries to provide a source of understanding and guidance. Consider the following examples from the Edgar Cayce readings. In each case the interpretation is straightforward and clear. The source of each dream seems to be something within the dreamer that wants to help and is worth befriending. The reader is encouraged not to be too concerned with the dream interpretation technique Edgar Cayce is using in these examples (there will be ample material on this in the rest of the book), but rather to recognize the way in which the unconscious mind demonstrates its willingness to cooperate with the dreamer as a *helpful, directive influence toward self-understanding.*

Q-1. [I dreamed of a] leak of what seemed to be liquor on our foyer rug, out of a bottle . . . or keg.
A-1. . . . .As is seen, this is as the warning to the entity as respecting liquors in and about the place, and in the use of same let them be used in discretion, that there be not the harm . . . that is, let not these conditions become the stumbling block, either to health, position, or influential surroundings, see?
137-97

Q-3. [I dreamed that] a dummy with a blue lady's suit and no head was sitting on our day bed.

A-3. . . .Let not those associations of the entity become such as is viewed. Rather seek the association, the counsel and advice, of those who are not as dummies.   137-97

Q-1. . . .Please interpret the dream I had the night of May 1st or 2nd in which a member of Group #1 and I were climbing a mountain and later I was separated from her and could not find her.

A-1. . . .In this, it arises from seeking and, as is understood, it is an emblematical experience in the mental development. . . Through that vision it may be seen that the mountain represents the reaching higher and higher in the mental development of self and those associated with self, that in climbing these heights of mental or spiritual experiences there come separations; which is not to be wondered at, but rather as experienced.   262-64

Q-3. [I dreamed] I was giving out dollar bills to people, one at a time. One person would come up to me and say, "Give me one." I would hand that person a dollar, then another would come up, and another and another.

A-3. [Emblematical] of the great truths that the entity. . .is to hand out to those who seek a more perfect understanding of their relations with their Creator, for as the representation of dollars to the material mind is of that success in a material world, these are the emblematical forces and are but as the grains of truth as are to be handed out.   900-109

In each of these dreams as interpreted by Edgar Cayce there is evidence of a gentle, yet purposeful influence for selfunderstanding. Something within each of these dreamers was showing its willingness to cooperate with the growth needs of that individual.

The development of *cooperation* is the first stage in a special growth sequence proposed in the Cayce readings, a sequence that is applicable to our work with dreams and to almost any other endeavor. A careful examination of the meaning of cooperation will reveal that it is actually far more than merely the ability to get along with others or a begrudging willingness to compromise. The clearest definition of this quality, according to the Edgar Cayce readings, is found in Chapter 1 (fittingly entitled "Cooperation") of *A Search for God*. This twovolume book was written over an eleven-year period by a small group of friends of Edgar Cayce who regularly received readings on spiritual development. Those readings—130 in all—outlined a 24-lesson growth sequence for spiritual, mental and physical unfoldment. As just stated, cooperation was given as the first stage in that sequence; an individual's further growth depends largely on his or her capacity to experience the meaning of cooperation, which is defined in the *Search for God* text as follows:

> "Cooperation in the physical is defined as acting or operating jointly with others, concurring with others in action or effort. In the spiritual it is more. It is losing sight of self and becoming a channel through which blessings may flow to others. The blessing is cooperation in action. Whether in the spiritual or physical, action is necessary to put cooperation into operation." *A Search for God,* Book I, p. 23

In essence, then, we have a two-part definition. From the physical perspective, cooperation is "concurring with [another] in action or effort." If we examine the relationship between the unconscious and the conscious selves, we see that cooperation of this nature takes place as the unconscious mind considers the needs of the conscious self and makes the "effort" to produce a dream. In this case, "effort" is not meant to imply "exertion"—for the dream is a very natural product of the unconscious—but simply the "action" of creating the dream.

From the spiritual perspective, cooperation is "becoming a channel through which blessings may flow. . ." Once again considering the relationship between the unconscious and the conscious selves, we find that cooperation of this nature takes place as the spiritual forces express themselves in a dream, providing guidance and understanding (i.e., blessings) to the conscious self.

However, this illustrates only how the unconscious cooperates with the conscious in the creation of dream experiences. A reciprocal cooperation is required if we are to experience fully the value of dreams. In other words, we need to find an approach to cooperating with and befriending our own unconscious minds.

Using the two-part definition from *A Search for God,* we conclude that there may be specific actions or efforts that we can make to develop a closer relationship to our dream world. These efforts might include the use of suggestion before we go to sleep, procedures to enhance dream recall, and the discipline of keeping a dream journal. These will be discussed in detail in the next section of this chapter.

Futhermore, we conclude that to cooperate with our dreams we must adopt an attitude of desiring to be a channel through which blessings may flow. However, being a channel is not passive; the blessings flow as we put into action what we receive. In other words, to truly cooperate with our dreams we must be prepared to do more than just write them down and analyze them. Cooperation will mean putting their lessons into action in daily life. We will see that this is an integral part of the Edgar Cayce readings' notion of dream interpretation. It is suggested in the following question-and-answer exchange.

Q-9. . . .*Will I be able to prophesy through dreams?*
A-9. Rather interpret.
Q-10. . . .*Will I be able to interpret those that come through me?*
A-10. If thou will only open self to be a channel.   262-5

Conscious Efforts at Cooperating with Dreams

We cannot work very effectively with our dreams unless we are remembering them. Fortunately, the readings give us some suggestions for enhancing dream recall. The first step is to have a clear understanding of what it is we are trying to remember. In Chapter 1, a part of our definition of a dream was "an actual experience of the soul." A remembered dream is rarely the direct experience itself. Instead, it is a representation of the experience in tems of a vocabulary which is recognizable to our conscious minds and which consists primarily of images, thoughts and memories. The process of bringing back the impression of an actual experience is described in the readings in the following manner.

. . .when such an action [of the soul and spiritual forces] is of such a nature as to make or bring back imprssions to the conscious mind in the earth or material plane, it is termed a dream.   3744-4

As is implied in this passage, not all the experiences of the soul during sleep are brought back as dream impressions. Conceivably, even the person who remembers six or seven dreams on a given night may not have brought back impressions of all the experiences of his or her soul during that sleep period. Furthermore, not all impressions recalled the next morning can properly be called dreams. Apparently, the mind is active throughout the night. We may awaken during the night with the remembrance of thinking about a particular subject. In this case what we have recalled is not a dream, but simply a type of conscious mental process that carried over into the sleep state. We have probably all had experiences of this nature, such as carrying into sleep a worry about something at our job. An authoritative discussion of this phenomenon can be found in *The Psychology of Dreaming,** in which Dr. Robert Van de Castle includes this definition of a dream: "...that type of mental [sleep] experience in which there is a vivid, perceptual experience frequently involving considerable emotion and bizarre, implausible events. .."

Despite the fact that not all the sleep experiences we remember are properly called dreams, there are specific things we can do to enhance the remembrance of valid dreams. The Cayce readings suggest two such procedures. The first is to make proper use of the hypnagogic state (i.e., that halfway state between sleeping and wakefulness). This is a level of consciousness that almost all people have noticed, either as they fall asleep or as they gradually wake up. It is characterized by vivid, dreamlike imagery, yet it often includes some degree of self-consciousness. This factor of self-awareness is usually missing in a typical dream. By paying attention to this hypnagogic state as one awakens in the morning, one can enhance dream recall. The hypnagogic state ends when one fully awakens, when one has a sense of being "in the physical body," and when the logical, rational mind once again becomes dominant. The phrase used for this in the Cayce readings is "the physical. . .gaining its equilibrium."

Dreams. . .should be made record of, else the physical in gaining its equilibrium often loses much that may be worthwhile. . . 294-46

In practical application this means taking time in the morning to pay attention to miscellaneous images and thoughts that arise as you wake up. It also means that dream recall is likely to be significantly hindered if you are jarred awake by an alarm or jump out of bed immediately upon awakening. When told that a few extra minutes of lying in bed may enhance dream recall, most people are more than happy to give it a try!

The second specific procedure for improving dream recall is to attune oneself to the spiritual forces. This is suggested in the following hypothesis: "As to those who are nearer the spiritual realm, their visions, dreams, and the like, are more often . . . retained by the individual. . ." (5754-3) Although this hypothesis has not yet been thoroughly tested in a systematic research setting, at least one study has shown results to support the concept. Dr. Henry Reed conducted a research

---

**The Psychology of Dreaming,* by Robert Van de Castle, Morristown, New Jersey: General Learning Press, 1971, p. 29.

project* in which more than 500 people submitted records of their dream experiences over a 28-day period. Dr. Reed found that on nights following days in which research participants had meditated before the sleep period, 66% of the participants evidenced improved dream recall.

We should each consider personally what procedures are most likely to enhance attunement to the spiritual forces. We may discover that this will involve changing our life style, and we may meet with resistance from our habit patterns. There is probably something within us all that would prefer a simple technique to enhance dream recall (like lying in bed an extra five minutes), because changing our life style sounds like quite a drastic measure. However, we can be assured that once we start *interpreting* those very dreams we want to remember, we are going to discover suggestins from the unconscious—quite strong or pointed suggestions—to make life style changes! Making basic changes for purposes of better recall at the very beginning of our work with dreams simply puts us ahead of the game. Those changes which can lead to better attunement include daily meditation, prayer, ample physical exercise and a balanced diet. To make this more immediately practical, we can say that a period of meditation, prayer, and/or devotional reading (e.g., the Bible) before going to sleep will aid in the remembrance of dreams.

In addition to these two basic procedures given in the readings, many other methods for improving recall have been suggested by people who work with their dreams. Among these practices are the following:

1. Go to bed early. Dream research indicates that *we all dream nightly* and that dreams come in a cyclical pattern. That is, most of our dreams happen in a sleep stage called REM, which is an abbreviation for Rapid Eye Movement. These REM periods recur throughout the night, mingled with the other stages of sleep. Our first REM period is likely to be brief (typically 4 to 6 minutes). Our second one, usually about 90 minutes later, will probably last a bit longer (8 to 12 minutes). This pattern continues throughout the night, with each REM period occurring about 90 minutes after the end of the last one and with each successive REM period likely to be longer than the preceding one. By the eighth hour of sleep we are probably having quite a lengthy dream period. If we cut ourselves short on sleep time for a given night, we have probably cut out our longest dream period.

---

*See *Sundance Community Dream Journal,* 1976, Vol. I, No. 1, available from A.R.E. Press, P.O. Box 595, Virginia Beach, VA 23451.

2. Have a partner wake you during REM periods. This technique is especially helpful for the person who has extreme difficulty remembering his dreams. It requires a dedicated partner who does not mind missing some sleep to help a friend catch a dream. Basically, all the partner has to do is sit by the bed (with a dim light in the room, of course, or the whole effort will be in vain) and watch the sleeping person's closed eyelids. When a REM period begins, the watcher will observe the eyeballs moving under the eyelids. After allowing this to proceed for several minutes, the watcher should awaken the dreamer—gently—with the question, "What were you dreaming?"

3. Learn to awaken in the night. We are much more likely to remember a dream if we awaken just after it occurs. Therefore, a person who sleeps through the entire night without even once awakening is probably less inclined to remember a dream, other than the last dream of the sleep cycle. Although it may seem very annoying to some people to have to awaken during the night, most serious dream recorders find it helpful.

There are at least two ways to increase the likelihood of such awakenings. The first is to *train* oneself to awaken at a particular time. Most of us have learned to do this for our morning awakening, and the habit probably persists, even on weekend mornings when we can sleep late. A simple procedure—although admittedly not an especially attractive one—is to set an alarm to go off during the night. Some time between 2:00 A.M. and 5:00 A.M. is best for most people. A radio alarm that produces music is probably preferable to a harsh buzzer. However, the purpose of the alarm is not to catch the dream, but rather to begin to train the mind to awaken *on its own* at that time. Some people are fortunate with this procedure and recall a dream when the alarm awakens them; others find the alarm—even if it is music—to be such a shock that any dream is lost because of the rapid arousal. People in the latter group should work with the alarm for a matter of days and then see if the training has worked. Some individuals will find that after a period of such training they awaken on their own at that middle-of-the-night time and frequently recall a dream that probably would have been missed otherwise.

A second way to increase the likelihood of awakening in the night to recall a dream is to drink one or two glasses of water before going to bed. The body's desire to urinate will probably cause an awakening during the night. Again, this procedure might be used merely as a training method to develop a natural habit of awakening from sleep after a dream.

4. If you awaken during the night, write down just one or two key words describing any dream you remember. This technique

is an effective aid to total dream recall in the morning. Most of us have probably had the experience of awakening in the night with a clearly remembered dream, saying to ourselves, "Now there is no way I could forget this one," and going back to sleep—only to find that we cannot remember the dream the next morning. There is a good compromise between the lengthy process of writing out the entire dream at 3:00 A.M. and acting on the unreliable conclusion that the memory will still be with us in the morning. We can simply write down a few key characters or symbols from the dream. Having a pad of paper by the bedside makes this quite simple. However, this technique should not be understood to imply that a dream journal is not required. The compromise to avoid having to write out the entire dream applies only to those sleepy moments in the middle of the night when a dream is first recalled. It is to be hoped that the next morning the dreamer will be able to use those few key words to bring back the entire memory and will carefully record the details of the dream.

5. Read your dream journal account of recent dreams before going to bed. This is one good pre-sleep activity that will enhance dream recall. It might be seen as an effort to "prime the pump." Not only does it get the mind focused upon the dream life just before sleep, but in addition it may increase the possibility of dreams which repeat the message of the previous night. Later we shall see that a series of dreams concerning a particular lesson or life problem makes a proper interpretation more likely. In reading the previous dreams before going to sleep, an individual may wish to (1) simply read the content of the dreams, (2) try reliving or re-experiencing the dreams in his or her imagination, or (3) work on interpreting the dreams.

6. Before going to sleep, use a simple suggestion for dream recall. Later in this chapter we will examine more carefully the use of sleep suggestion to nurture a particular quality of dream experience. However, the mind is also susceptible to suggestion related to remembering dreams. This technique is easily completed: as you are falling asleep, repeat to yourself several times, "I will remember my dreams upon awakening." This suggestion does not have to be the very last thought of the night in order for it to work. What is most important is the sincerity of feeling and desire behind the suggestion. The words are not a magic incantation; they work only to the degree that we really do want to remember our dreams.

7. Keep paper, pencil and flashlight by your bed. This technique has already been referred to in the paragraph on writing down a few key dream symbols. In keeping these items by the bed, we provide a powerful suggestion to the mind that

we are, in fact, serious about the business of remembering and working with our dreams.

8. Record your feelings upon awakening, even if you recall no dreams. This is an especially effective tool for the person who rarely remembers a dream. Its value lies in the discipline of paying attention to inner states—in this case, feelings—and appreciating them enough to commit them to paper. Often after several days or weeks of this the person who has had poor dream recall will begin to remember dream fragments or single symbols which accompany the feelings. By maintaining the discipline to record just these feelings or fragments the individual can eventually learn to catch a lengthy dream. The following is an example entry in a journal record of mere feelings upon awakening:

"This morning I awakened earlier than usual and feeling quite at peace with myself. My thoughts seemed quite naturally to turn to B [a friend] and I seemed to have quite a positive attitude towards him when compared to yesterday."

9. Record and study other dreamlike fantasies. Many people who have had trouble remembering dreams have found they are helped through intentional fantasy exercises. These can take many forms, including music reverie or daydreaming. A simple example of this approach is applicable to mornings when one does not recall a dream. Merely taking a few moments lying in bed and allowing the mind to wander into a daydream or fantasy can produce imagery that can be recorded in a journal, much as one would write down a normal dream. Some people find it worth while to study and try to interpret such fantasy or daydream experiences in the same way they would work with a dream. A case could be made against treating such experiences as we would dreams; however, their value may lie most directly in stimulating a deeper awareness of inner, subjective impressions, and thus making it more likely that actual dreams will be recalled the next night.

10. Upon awakening, review the key questions in your life. This method of enhancing dream recall has been proposed by Dr. Herbert Puryear. It is based on the assumption that we tend to dream about the things for which we have concern in waking life. The first step in this procedure is to make a list of four to ten significant questions or concerns that you currently face (e.g., "Should I look for a new job?" or "What should I do to help my child who is failing in his schoolwork?"). The individual is encouraged first to make a record of those dreams that are immediately recalled upon awakening in the morning. Once this is done, the next step is to try to stimulate awareness of dreams that might otherwise remain forgotten. This can be accomplished by asking oneself the questions which have been

previously listed. For example, "Did I have a dream about vocation or changing jobs last night?" or "Did I have a dream about my child or about schoolwork last night?"

Occasionally we may find that upon posing a specific question of this nature we suddenly remember a dream, but the dream seemingly has nothing to do with the question. Although we should not rule out the possibility that it was merely an accident that the recall came at that moment, a good place to start working with such a dream is to explore how it could conceivably be related to the question just posed.

11. Write out your purposes for wanting to recall dreams. For most, if not all, individuals, the ability to remember dreams is related to the motivations behind doing so. Why do you want to remember your dreams? Is it merely curiosity or a desire to impress others with your unusual experiences? Or is it related to a sincere desire to understand yourself or be able to be a better person. Deciding upon our motivation for working with dreams is an aspect of setting ideals, a topic to be examined more closely in a later chapter. In regard to dream recall, some people have found clarifying their purposes for wanting to remember dreams to be a helpful step. In some cases individuals have found that their motivation or purpose did not seem very worth while. When that purpose was changed, dream recall began to occur more often.

12. Pray for recall yourself, or have others pray for you. It is easy to become very technique-oriented and forget this most direct aid for remembering dreams. By sincerely praying for understanding through dreams, we are attuning ourselves to the spiritual forces within. The prayers of others for us (when we have asked for such help) can also aid this attunement. And, as we have seen, a fundamental notion in the Cayce readings on dreaming is that attunement of the body and mind to the spirit will be helpful for remembering dreams.

13. Have an inquiring attitude. It is interesting to note that in many of the Cayce dream readings the initial words are, "We have the inquiring mind of. . ." Apparently this quality of seeking was necessary for an effective dream interpretation to be given. We can nurture such a quality most directly by making a study of the literature on dreams. In other words, a consistent effort to read books and articles on dreams and dream theory will enhance our sense of having an inquiring mind and is likely to increase our access to the dream world through recall.

14. Act on the dreams you receive. This is an extremely practical and effective way to develop from an occasional dream recaller into a frequent one. By applying the lessons and

guidance we find in our dreams, we are likely to move towards *greater attunement*—which will in itself increase recall—and we will be *investing energy* in a process that links the inner world more firmly to the outer world.

In summary, we have examined briefly fourteen specific techniques and approaches to enhance recall of dreams. So many people report trouble in remembering their dreams that it would probably be worth while to take one more look at a list of these fourteen items. There is certainly no lack of things to try if you are having trouble in this area! These are all ways in which we can make an effort to develop a more cooperative relationship with our unconscious minds.

Going to bed early	Recording feelings upon awakening
Having a partner watch for REM	Recording fantasies
Learning to awaken in the night	Reviewing life questions
Recording one key symbol	Writing out purposes
Reading previous dreams (or journal writing)	Praying
Using simple sleep suggestion	Developing an inquiring mind
Having paper and pen by the bed	Acting on dreams

Keeping a Dream Journal

Dream recall is a delicate and elusive thing. A dream which seems quite vivid in the morning may easily become quite hazy by the end of the day. Since, due to time requirements such as getting to work, the morning frequently is not the best time to work on dream interpretation, a careful record of our dream experiences is extremely important. Some people have found that it is only weeks or months after a particular dream has occurred that they are able to unlock its meaning. Without having written down such a dream, an interpretation probably would not be possible.

A second important reason for recording our dreams concerns the necessity of bringing the lessons of such inner experiences into daily application. The very act of recording a dream—whether in words or in a drawing—is the first step in giving it physical manifestation. To some degree this means that committing a dream to paper is a symbolic act which says to ourselves, "I intend to work on understanding this dream and on bringing its message into physical expression."

Of course, the initial step in keeping a dream journal is to find a suitable volume. Many people find a spiral notebook quite suitable and inexpensive. Others prefer a looseleaf notebook or a bound book with blank pages. No matter what you choose, you may find it helpful to write your dreams on only the right-hand pages of the opened book, leaving the left-hand pages for comments and notes about possible interpretations. This method is especially valuable because it allows one to write an interpretive comment alongside the dream narration at the appropriate point.

Three other factors should be considered in keeping a dream journal. A brief resumé of the previous day's events, thoughts and feelings—those things that, in our definitions of dreams in the previous chapter, were called the mental forces—may be very helpful in later work on interpretation. Typically, a 20- to 50-word summation is sufficient. Giving the dream a title may also be quite useful in dream study. To determine a title for a particular dream we simply try to find a phrase that summarizes what the dream is about. Finally, in keeping a dream journal we should make an effort to record all the details of the dream, even those events or symbols that do not seem very important at the time. In the dream state we often misjudge which events and scenes presented to us in the dream are most important. In the following example a brief dream is recorded using the style which has just been described.

October 29, 1977
Yesterday I awakened late and had to hurry to work. Routine day except for argument with Richard. Home by 5:30. Went out to eat at a Chinese restaurant. Watched TV for 1 hour (football game). To bed at 11:00.

"College Friend Reunion"

Campus—learning?
youth?

I am back on the campus where I went to college. I see John and Bob and we get into my car to go to a restaurant. I finish first and go out to the car. It seems as if they have

"feeling forgotten" perhaps relevant to current life situations. Dream perhaps encourages me to try to contact these two friends again.

forgotten me because they don't come out. I keep thinking I should have asked them what they've been doing these past 10 years.

Dream Incubation and Sleep Suggestion

A further way in which we can develop a more cooperative relationship with the unconscious mind is through efforts to nurture a particular quality of dream experience. Most often this procedure is used to enlist a dream to help answer a specific problem or question. The notion of "incubating" a dream is an ancient one, used in an especially effective manner in the Greek dream temples of the god Aesculapius. Citizens of that ancient society who required guidance on personal medical problems would go through elaborate procedures designed to stimulate dreams in response to their needs. Those who were guiding the dreamer through these incubation procedures would help him in the interpretation and application of the dream message.

In modern times several dream researchers have used adaptations of these ancient concepts. One noteworthy example is Dr. Henry Reed, whose work is described in his article entitled "Dream Incubation."*

One element of nearly all modern forms of dream incubation is the use of suggestion as the dreamer falls asleep. Of course, suggestions can be of a wide variety and are not limited merely to words that are repeated as one is going to sleep. For example, sleeping in a room with pictures of famous movie monsters on the walls might be considered a suggestive influence for a certain quality of dream. In general, we can say that sleep suggestion includes (1) anything available to the sensory system before going to sleep, and (2) subjective impressions and memories stimulated before falling asleep. In the light of this definition, it is clear that every night we receive sleep suggestions that are likely to affect our dreams!

The Edgar Cayce readings frequently mention the influence of suggestion on dreaming. In the first of the passages below, we find the idea that suggestion can be used to stimulate guidance in our dreams. In the second and third passages, we find the concept that suggestion is a powerful influence upon the content of dreams; and furthermore, the nature of that influence is summed up in the phrase "Like begets like."

[Dreams] may be developed to that point where the subconscious will give the directing way, through suggestions to same in the subjugated state of consciousness, see?136-18

[Dreams] vary according to that suggestion given by the mental forces of the entity when the physical consciousness is laid aside. . .   900-200

---

*Journal of Humanistic Psychology, Volume 16, 1976, pp. 53-70.

. . .as has been seen by even those attempting to produce a certain character of vision or dream—these follow much in that; for another law that is universal becomes active! Like begets like! 5754-3

There remains an important question we must ask ourselves about our use of suggestion specifically to try to incubate a dream about a problem or question: Are we attempting to force a dream experience in an unnatural way? In other words, are we actually trying to manipulate our dream world? If we are doing this, we are violating the fundamental theme of this chapter: *cooperation* with the unconscious. However, properly understood and practiced, the use of sleep suggestion to incubate dream guidance is not manipulation. This is evident if we realize that the subconscious and spiritual forces within us *naturally seek expression* in a manner that will be helpful to our conscious physical selves. What gets in the way of this expression is usually our conscious desires or distracting thought patterns. In this sense, sleep suggestion is directed not so much to the subconscious and spiritual forces, but rather to the mental forces (i.e., our conscious selves). Dream incubation through suggestion is therefore the conscious, cooperative effort on our part to *allow our dreams to do what they naturally want to do.* This is stated clearly in the Cayce readings:

The dreams, as we see, come nearer and nearer, *when allowed to do so,* to that inner consciousness that may be brought to the oneness. . . 900-174

The actual mechanics of using suggestion to get dream guidance are quite simple and straightforward. First, we pose the question we want answered, preferably writing it out in a dream journal. It is usually important to phrase the question in such a way that it can be answered yes or no. For example, rather than asking, "Whom should I marry?" the question should be either, "Is it best for me to be married at this time in my life?" or "Am I right in wanting to marry Jane Smith?"

Next, we should make a tentative conscious decision regarding the question. Since a part of our work in the earth as spiritual beings is to *learn* to make decisions in keeping with God's will, we need this practice. We do not learn how to do this by turning our decision-making over to the unconscious. Rather, what we seek is guidance or feedback from a more unlimited perspective (i.e., dreams) on the course we have consciously chosen. It may be a good idea to write down our tentative conscious decision in the dream journal right next to the question.

A period of meditation and prayer just before going to bed will be very helpful in this incubation process. Then, as you fall asleep, simply review the question and your tentative decision. Since one of the functions of a dream is to tune in to what has already been set in motion, the dream which you may experience that night is likely to give you feedback on what probably will follow if you carry out your tentative decision. Based upon that dream feedback, you may choose to change your decision. For example, if you consciously decide to marry Jane Smith and then have dreams of the two of you bickering and not getting along, you may want to reconsider your decision.

In working with this procedure, there are two things we want to keep in mind: persistence and sincerity. Frequently, it takes several nights before we get a dream that seems to include guidance or feedback on our tentative decision. In addition, it is not just curiosity that makes this procedure work. When asked in a reading how to determine whether or not a particular dream was in fact answering a posed question, Cayce answered "No" and that "When he desires it sufficiently, then, not just wishes for [the dream answer], it will come." (195-31)

A final thought on sleep suggestion and dream incubation concerns the reliability of the answer we get. How can we be sure that the unconscious is truly cooperating? One step which should always be taken in answering this is *to measure* the guidance received in comparison to the highest ideal we have for our lives. In other words, we ask ourselves, "Does this guidance direct me to act in a way that is consistent with the *best* I know about life?" If the answer is no, we should start the guidance-seeking process over again from the beginning.

However, even if the above question can be answered in the affirmative, this does not necessarily mean that we have properly understood the dream. A clear example of this can be seen in the present writer's own experience. Having graduated from college, I was concerned about when I would find a place to work. My first choice was an organization on the east coast. I had met several of the staff members of that organization and was greatly impressed with their ideals and work. I made a tentative conscious decision to move to that area and seek employment with that group. I then turned to prayer and dreams, hoping for some guidance.

Shortly thereafter, I had a dream in which I was talking with a staff member of that organization. We discussed the possibility of my coming to work there. When I awakened, the last thing I remembered in the dream was that he told me "No," there would not be a job and I had best not come. Because of that dream, I changed my decision and set in motion an alternative plan, aimed at obtaining employment elsewhere.

However, about one week later I had a second dream. In this one I was walking along the sidewalk and saw the same man approaching. I called to him and told him that I had dreamed of him recently (i.e., the first dream). He responded, "Oh, yes, I remember that dream. But *you* didn't remember the whole thing." He then proceeded to tell me how the first dream had actually ended. He explained that upon carefully reviewing my past experiences he had changed his mind, and in fact there would be a job available for me. In this second dream he also mentioned what my job title would be and the date when the job would start (some nine months later).

Basing my decision upon the second dream, I changed my plans again, moved to the area of this organization, and was finally hired. The job I was offered was almost identical to the one described in the dream, and the starting date was within seven days of the one mentioned. In addition to having been of obvious personal value, this dream sequence also points out that if we will simply *act on the best we know* from our dreams, there is a feedback loop that will correct our course if we have misunderstood the guidance or lesson. However, without our willingness to make initial efforts at applying the best we know, this feedback loop is blocked.

Chapter Three
THE BASICS OF DREAM INTERPRETATION

Almost everyone is fascinated by the notion that the seeming nonsense of most dreams can have an underlying meaning. One Jewish tradition likens a dream uninterpreted to a letter unopened; just as we are all excited to open and read a letter from a friend, we are intrigued by the idea of discovering a hidden, secret message in our dreams. In this case, however, the letter is from ourselves—although a forgotten part of ourselves.

Sigmund Freud offered a basic approach to dream interpretation that involves reversing the process that goes into the creation of the dream. Since the message of the dream, in his opinion, is usually something unacceptable to the conscious mind, it has to be disguised in order to pass through the censor of the ego. This process of disguising the message in symbolic form is called dream work. Hence dream interpretation becomes simply a matter of undoing or unraveling the dream work.

Carl Jung took a different view of the basics of dream interpretation. At the root of his psychological approach was the concept that the human soul is in the process of unfoldment. This process of growth in consciousness could ultimately culminate in what Jung called "individuation." A key principle for our discussion of dream interpretation is that Jung saw the possibility of profound wisdom and insight coming from the unconscious. Frequently a particular level of understanding is available to the unconscious but is not yet understandable to the conscious mind. For this reason, the message or lesson is portrayed in symbols.

In the dream interpretations given in the Cayce readings we find some elements in common with the Freudian approach and others that are consistent with the Jungian. Some of the Cayce interpretations involve a message or a perspective of oneself to which the dreamer had been reluctant to admit. In these cases the unacceptable fact was much less frequently related to repressed sexual desires than had been claimed in

Freud's writing. In other Cayce interpretations we find evidence that wisdom or a higher perspective of life was being offered in symbolic form through the dream.

Purposes of and Attitudes Toward Interpretation

Several other significant factors are part of Cayce's overall approach to interpreting dreams. First is the insistence upon the necessity of a proper purpose or frame of mind for working with the dream. The following passage suggests what that attitude might be.

> In this particular experience, then, the body must approach this with the correct purpose, if same would be given in the way and manner that would be understood by the body. While this may be explained, or unraveled—as it were—for the consciousness of the entity, the whole reaction must be solely within self, if the body would be able to apply that gained through the experience. For remember, these are as illustrations only, and not means of an escape. . .   4167-1

The essential point appears to be one of *personal responsibility*. The passage suggests that the interpretation about to be given will be understood by the dreamer only if he takes responsibility for the message coming from his own inner self (i.e., "the whole reaction must be solely within self. . ."). Although the advisability of this may seem obvious, it points out one of the psychological problems of having someone else interpret our dreams, even if that person is as credible a source as Edgar Cayce. Once we have looked outside ourselves for the message of the dream, we may continue to look outside ourselves for the solution or application which the dream points out. Expecting someone else to do things in response to our own dreams may be an example of the warned-against "means of an escape. . ." For example, imagine that a man is having marital difficulties but is unable to determine the root of the problem. He goes to a counselor and together they work on interpreting his dreams. In one session the counselor interprets a dream to mean that the man is unconsciously harboring resentments toward something his wife did years ago. Assuming that the interpretation is correct, the real test is how the dreamer will respond. Having had the dream analyzed for him, will he look to the counselor for the solution to the resentment instead of taking personal responsibility for this needed healing? Will he tell the dream to his wife and expect her to make the changes necessary to mend the relationship? If he follows this course, he is using the dream as a "means of an escape. . ." He is escaping from personal responsibility by saying, in effect, "My dream has revealed to me that I am a victim of unconscious conditions controlling my life." Even though this dream has been "interpreted" after a fashion and the dreamer has come to understand himself a bit better, he is not really the better for it.

Defining Interpretation

This imaginary case points out the need for a deeper understanding of what interpreting a dream should involve. To get a truer picture of what should go into an effective dream *interpretation,* we can turn to another area of experience in which this term is used—foreign languages. The readings even suggest this analogy by referring to dreams as the speech of the unconscious: ". . .all dreams are but the speech of the conditions in the mental, physical, or subconscious self." (900-8)

Imagine three individuals. One speaks only Italian; the second, only English; and the third, both languages. What criterion should we use to evaluate how effective an interpreter the third individual is? What would be required is not just a literal, word-by-word translation. Even though that might be helpful, it would miss much of the subtlety of what is being communicated. Instead, the fundamental requirement for a good language interpreter is the capacity to take the essence of a living, meaningful experience being communicated by one person and transmit it to another in a different form but one that retains its living, meaningful nature. In this analogy, the first individual can represent the dream world; the second person, the world of daily life; and the third individual, our conscious efforts to make sense out of our remembered dreams.

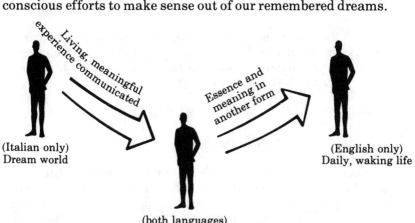

Living, meaningful experience communicated

Essence and meaning in another form

(Italian only)
Dream world

(both languages)
Effective dream interpreter

(English only)
Daily, waking life

This analogy suggests that we fail to truly interpret a dream when we arrive at only a mental formulation of what the dream means. Far too often this is what students of dreams want to do—obtain the solution to the dream puzzle. It is as if once we have figured out what the dream is saying we can write the message down in our dream journal, put a gold star next to that dream, and move on to the next one. At best this approach is mere dream translation—translating the symbolic representation or language into a more verbal, intellectual format. However, it is not dream interpretation. Instead, we should define dream interpretation as our *response through application in daily life to the living, meaningful experience remembered from the dream world.*

This definition rests upon the theory of learning found in the Cayce readings. The essence of that theory is that only in the application and experience of a principle do we really understand it. In other words, only as we apply the message of a dream, as best we understand it at that moment, do we truly interpret it. This concept is clearly stated in the following two passages.

> ...as these lessons as gained from [dreams] are applied in the daily life, there comes the more consciousness of the truths as are shown in the same; for in *doing* there comes the understanding. 900-322

> The dreams, as we see, come to the entity through those channels as have been outlined for the entity, and are to be applied in the physical, the mental, and the spiritual life, as experiences for the development of the entity; for in experience and in application only are the truths set forth...
> 900-374

With this perspective of dream interpretation, we will want to include in our dream journals not only the mental solution of what a dream means, but also a record of the specific steps we take to apply that dream message in daily life.

Who Is the Best Interpreter?

Having developed this definition of dream interpretation, we should not be surprised that the Cayce readings suggest we are our own best interpreters. One reading even warned against becoming too dependent upon dream interpretation books (such as this one) or upon the opinions of others.

Q-5. What is meant in my life reading by the statement that I would have imposing dreams and how can I best interpret them to be helpful to me in the present?
A-5. These have come, these may come. Ye interpret them in thyself. Not by dream book, not by what others say, but dreams are presented in symbols, in signs. 1968-10

The *body* may analyze same [dreams], interpret same, *better;* for it can do it better for its own activity than were it done by the most wonderful of all interpreters. And so may it be given to all. 257-138

As we have given respecting visions or experiences of individuals, they in themselves may be the better interpreters of their experiences; provided, to be sure, there is the attempt, the desire in each to know, and the willingness to be guided or directed by those influences. 262-41

The third passage is noteworthy in that it puts a stipulation on the answer to who is the best interpreter. If we are sincere in our efforts and desires, and if we are open to the possibility of guidance from within, we can work with our own dreams better than anyone else can—even better than a "wonderful" source such as the Cayce readings themselves.

There are at least three reasons why it is better for us to depend on ourselves for interpretations. First, if interpretation means application of the message of the dream, then it is obvious that no one else can do this for us. Second, the language of dreams is one of symbols, and each person has personal associations with various symbolic images. The meaning of a particular dream symbol often relates to how the dreamer personally feels or reacts to it. It is unlikely that someone else knows the dreamer's own attitudes and tastes better than he does. Frequently when someone else interprets a dream what that person is actually doing is saying what the dream would mean if he had had it. However, since the dreamer and the outside interpreter may have some common ground of experience, the interpretation offered may occasionally be an accurate one. Of course, the possibility of psychic perception by the outside interpreter makes it more likely that the two do have a common ground of experience. Also, the psychic is probably less likely to block or reject an interpretation which the dreamer would find painful or unacceptable. Why, then, we might ask, do the Cayce readings imply that not even a gifted psychic is a better interpreter than the dreamer himself?

The answer to this question is the third reason for the advisability of personal dream work. An extremely valuable part of working with dreams is the actual *process* itself of

39

unraveling the dream message. Our growth and unfoldment in consciousness certainly comes as we apply the dream in daily life, but it also comes as we go through the inner wrestling and playing with the dream images and events.

Anyone who has tutored someone in mathematics or physics has probably discovered this principle. It is not as important for the student to get the right solution on his homework as it is for him to learn the process by which that solution can be found. The truly effective tutor is the one who can ask the right questions of the student, allowing him to discover for himself the proper steps to take in order to find the solutions. The pupil who simply watches the tutor work all the problems for him will never achieve the desired results. He himself needs to be able to solve similar problems on an exam when there is no tutor around to help.

This analogy should be instructive concerning our desire to help another person with his dreams. If we really want to be helpful, we will appreciate the value of the *process* of unlocking the dream. We will ask questions, such as "What does that particular symbol mean to you?" or "In what other ways might you have responded to what was happening in the dream?" Only as a last resort will we try to interpret the dream directly, and then only with qualifying statements like "If this were my own dream I would think it meant this."

Symbology

Our first tendency in working with a dream may be to attempt the translation of its symbols. However, when doing this we must be very careful to appreciate the meaning of symbology itself. A symbol is *far more* than just an emblem or sign which represents something that we already consciously know. Even though the form or image of a dream symbol may resemble something familiar from daily life, it represents something deeper than its obvious meaning. The depth of that meaning is something that the conscious mind does not yet fully understand. Carl Jung's definition states that a symbol is the best possible representation of a complex fact not yet grasped by consciousness. Since it points to something that is not yet grasped, the symbol indicates the potential for growth in awareness.

In this sense we can talk about a symbol as something that is alive. Since our conscious minds have not yet fully understood the meaning or truth behind it, it is still a part of our ongoing unfoldment in awareness. In fact, we rarely are able to translate such an image and extract the fullness of its meaning and purpose. Usually, when we think we have done so we have actually failed to discover the richness of the dream. In those unusual instances in which we do finally grasp consciously the complex fact being represented, the symbol ceases to be alive for us. We may, in fact, find that once we have totally solved the mystery of a particular image it ceases to appear in our dreams. This points out the limited effectiveness of creating a personal dream-symbol list, *if* we treat that list as if it were a dictionary. We can, of course, keep a record of our latest understanding of particular symbols. But when we are finally successful at determining the exact definition of one of them, we find that that dictionary entry is of little use to us because the symbol is then dead.

Some students of dreams may not be pleased to read these notions of symbology. It is understandably frustrating to have the seemingly valuable tool of a symbology dictionary taken away. We can seem almost lost without it, as we travel through the apparent nonsense of most dreams. However, to truly grow in consciousness through dreams we must appreciate the fact that *the unconscious mind is not simply a hidden version of the conscious mind.* The unconscious operates with the calculus of the universe and cannot always be translated to the arithmetic of our conscious selves. We must grow slowly into the higher mathematics of life. We must patiently deal with the paradox of trying to apply a dream message and knowing at the same time that only a fraction of its deepest meaning has been touched.

Perhaps for these reasons, Edgar Cayce only infrequently approached a dream interpretation by translating the symbolic into the conscious concepts. Admittedly, there are instances in which he did this, yet there are far more in which he used alternative methods. This is not to say that the readings ignore the value of symbology, but rather that there seems to be a healthy respect for the fact that symbols are not unveiled by a simple wave of a wand (even a psychic one!). In spite of their reserved use of straight symbol translation in interpreting dreams, the readings do offer some significant insights for working with symbols, especially the symbolic characters in a dream.

There are at least five broad categories of ways of working with a dream symbol. It is usually advisable to try most or all of these approaches on the symbology of a dream of which we are attempting to get a thorough understanding.

The symbol literally represents what it appears to be. In other words, if I dream about John, it may actually be telling me something about him. If I dream about my automobile, I may be getting some clairvoyant guidance about its condition. In this regard, the Cayce readings make a major contribution to the literature of dream study. Whereas many psychologists view the notion of literal interpretation of a symbol to be quite naive—perhaps a reversion to primitive beliefs—recent dream telepathy research suggests that this type of symbology may indeed be valid. A later chapter includes a careful look at how to work with dreams that may literally be about the character they depict.

The symbol represents an aspect of the dreamer's personality. The majority of modern dream theorists adopt this viewpoint. In the case of a person who appears in our dream, this approach suggests that some part of ourselves is much like our perception of that person. A simple example of this would be to dream of a person whom we consider to be joyful. Perhaps that dream character symbolizes a part of ourselves (most likely a forgotten part) that has the quality of joy.

Interestingly, this way of interpreting dream characters is used *less frequently* in the Cayce readings than the first method. However, we should be careful not to draw conclusions too rigidly from the relative frequency of approaches used in the readings. For example, it is not clear that the dreams brought to Edgar Cayce constitute a representative sample of typical dreams. There may have been a tendency among those seeking readings to ask about only especially vivid or seemingly important ones. *Perhaps* (and this is only for the sake of speculative argument) the dreams that feel most important to us are the ones most likely to be literally about the persons they depict. All this is merely to say that we should not be too quick to undervalue the second approach simply because Cayce did not use it often. There are too many instances of fruitful dream work reported by people who use this second method for us to discount it. For those who have not tried this technique, it involves asking oneself, "What, to my mind, are the primary characteristics of this person?" or "If I were this person, how would I feel about life or myself?"

In using this second approach to understand nonhuman symbols, the dreamer seeks to determine personal associations or memories he may have in regard to that image. For example, in interpreting a dream about his automobile, one would ask questions such as "What kinds of memories do I have about automobiles?" or "When I hear the word automobile, what do I think of first?" The answers to these or similar questions may give us a clue as to which attitudes, memories or aspects of our personality are being represented.

The symbol represents a pattern of experience inherent in all human beings and therefore has approximately the same meaning for all people. This is the Jungian notion of archetypal symbology. In Jung's writing one finds the concept that most dream symbols come from a layer of the unconscious called the personal unconscious mind. This layer is somewhat like a storehouse of experiences for a particular individual. A symbol originating at this level may have a meaning which is relatively unique to the dreamer. For example, if one who is not especially fond of cats dreams of them, it probably has a different meaning than would a cat in the dream of a cat lover. We should note, however, that since within our culture we all live in similar, though not identical, social conditions and have many similar experiences, there *tends to be* similarity in how we interpret symbols from the personal unconscious mind. Unfortunately, this tendency breaks down once we compare ourselves to those of another society or culture.

Jung goes on to suggest that there are symbols that transcend even differences in culture. These symbols originate in a layer of mind he called the collective unconscious. The contents of this level of mind—accessible to and shared by all human beings—Jung called the *archetypes*. In other words, these are patterns of experiences and awareness that are written within us all simply because we are human. They are "givens." Just as the animal kingdom demonstrates that there are instincts of *behavior*, the archetypes may be instinctual types of consciousness within us all. Jung names many of them: the Wise Old Man, the Great Mother, the Shadow, the Trickster, the Christ. In dreams we can experience the collective unconscious and these archetypal patterns of awareness, and we bring back a remembrance of such experiences in terms of archetypal symbols: a white-haired benevolent man to represent that ancient source of wisdom within ourselves, the image of our own mother to represent the nurturing, caring aspect deep within us all.

As students of our own dreams, we would do well to study the work of researchers such as Jung who have discovered some of these archetypal symbols. Such research requires cross-cultural study of dreams, myths and architectural symbology. A reading list for the serious seeker might include some of Jung's own writing, such as *Archetypes and the Collective Unconscious,* and Joseph Campbell's multivolume work, *The Masks of God.*

A final note about archetypal symbols is important. Once we discover that a particular dream image *can potentially* be an archetype, that does *not* necessarily mean that every time it appears in a dream it has that meaning. For example, one's own mother could symbolize the Great Mother archetype, or it could symbolize a part of the dreamer similar to his mother or even literally depict the mother herself. In a later section we shall examine methods for determining the context in which a particular symbol is being used in a specific dream.

The symbol represents a quality that others would attribute to it. This possibility counterbalances the second one and, like it, suggests that the symbol represents an aspect of the dreamer himself. However, with this fourth approach a different method is used to determine just what that aspect might be. Rather than just asking "What are my personal feelings and associations with this symbolic image?" the dreamer might also ask himself, "What do *other people* associate with this image?"

For example, consider the hypothetical dream of a sporting goods salesman. Imagine that such a dream includes a rifle as one of its elements. When asked to make personal associations with this symbol, the dreamer is likely to equate it with a product that he sells to make a profit. In other words, generally speaking he has very positive associations with this image. On the other hand, this dreamer lives in a world made up of people who have a very different attitude towards rifles. Some people see them as instruments of destruction or harm. Because the dreamer frequently deals with such people and their attitudes in his daily life, the meaning of his dream symbol may reflect these other associations.

We may feel resistance to this notion and prefer to believe that our symbols are totally reflective of our own attitudes, beliefs and memories. However, there is a social dimension to daily life *and* to dream life. Just as many of our dreams give us literal insights into the characters that they depict, some of our symbols can be reflections of the attitudes and beliefs of those around us. Such a concept is found in the Biblical teaching to be our brother's keeper. Most likely we store, or "keep," within us the psychic makeup of those around us. When working with a dream symbol we should appreciate that some or all of its meaning may be tied to the associations that other people have with it.

The dream symbol represents a play on words or a pun. It is often fruitful to play with the symbols in a dream, looking for alternate meanings of the words (e.g., the symbol of a "pear" might represent a "pair of something"). Similarly, the action in a dream may depict some idiomatic phrase that has another meaning; for example, being "taken through the wringer" could represent the state of exhaustion. Or we can play with the words of symbols, expanding on them to discover what they may mean. Suppose, for instance, a person dreamed of a kite; he might expand this into the common phrase "high as a kite," and get a clue as to what it represents. The two passages below are examples of working with the elements of a dream in this way. In the first interpretaion Cayce indicates a pun on the name of one dream character. In the second case he suggests a play on the word "headless."

Q-1. . . .Great big mix-up and trouble. [900] was having trouble in Wabash and I saw Eugene Wolf and my Uncle Leo . . . in this connection. I was having trouble in New York, seemed to be with a party named Wolfe, on the New York Stock Exchange.
A-1. . . .This as is seen is related to that action as of the wolf, rather than man named Wolfe. That is, there has been in the trading in the exchange some individual who has acted in the wolfish-like manner, underhanded—apparently doing the entity a favor, yet taking advantage of knowledge of self. . .
137-41

Q-10. . . .A headless man in uniform of a sailor was walking in an erect manner with either a gun or a cane in his hand.
A-10. . . .then, to the entity the lesson: Do not lose the head too much in duty as seen, to accomplish the greater lessons as may be learned from the association of ideas as pertain to things more spiritual.
137-36

Summary of Symbology

We have seen that there are several potentially useful ways of working with a dream symbol. However, as attractive as having alternatives may be, it does present a problem in that almost any image that appears in a dream can seem to have multiple interpretations. Thus we are faced with the question of how to decide which of the many possibilities fits a specific symbol in a specific dream. The key to solving this problem is to determine the context in which the symbol appears. Several techniques described later in this book—notably, the theme approach found in the next chapter—can help us determine the context in which the symbol is used and therefore increase the likelihood that we will arrive at a proper meaning for it.

The phrase "*a proper meaning*" is carefully chosen, because it indicates our fundamental principle concerning symbols. No matter how effective the five approaches to working with dream images may be, we cannot escape our essential definition: a symbol represents something that the conscious self has not yet fully grasped. "A proper meaning" is therefore merely one that *leads us towards an application that will help us gain a better understanding of its message.*

Other Basic Principles of Interpretation

An important fact to realize about a dream is that it has two features. The first is the dream itself, with the images, events or voices perceived; in a sense, this is what is being presented by the inner forces. The second is the dreamer, the collection of his thoughts, reactions and responses to the dream. A basic principle of dream interpretation evident in the Cayce readings is that the dreamer does not always catch the significance or message of the dream. This is a subtle but invaluable point. The importance of the dreamer's responses will be explored in much greater depth in future chapters, especially the one entitled "Patience and the Dimensions of Dreaming."

One of the first writers to recognize the distinction between the dream and the dreamer is G. Scott Sparrow, who discusses it in his book, *Lucid Dreaming.** He points out that the dreamer is not infallible in his judgments while dreaming and frequently responds to the events of the dream in an entirely inappropriate way. As an example, consider the following dream:

We are outside, looking for hawks. I point to a distant hawk, which is carrying some game, and say that it looks like a falcon. As it nears, I realize with fear that it is a giant bee. I run to escape it. It chases me, and says over and over, "Let me give you light. Your parents have left your house without light or matches." I awaken in fear.

When awake, I realized that I had misinterpreted the intention of the bee. I sat up in bed and prayed that I might receive the gift it had offered to me.

This dream experience depicts the inner forces which seek to bring a blessing or a healing to the dreamer. However, the dreamer misinterprets what is really happening. Certainly we could examine the responses of the dreamer in this experience and learn much about him. However, we should not stop at that point and simply say that the dreamer has a lot of fear within him. We should also examine the dream itself, *irrespective of the responses of the dreamer.* A further example, taken from the readings, illustrates the same point.

Q-10. [I dreamed] words spoken: "You will drive to Deal by the 42nd Street Ferry." "But," I answered, "it has been set for us to go by 23rd Street Ferry—that is the way I have planned."

A-10. This, as we see, the warning to change plans as concerning the way and manner that they would go to Deal, for we will see with the coming of time why the change. This the presentation of that force that will guide, guard and protect...Be warned then not to go that way.   900-79

---

*Available from A.R.E. Press, P.O. Box 595, Virginia Beach, VA 23451.

In other words, the dream itself is relaying a valid message, but within the dream experience the dreamer fails to recognize the truth of what is being presented. We would not have arrived at the proper understanding of this dream if we had asked Mr. [900] a question like "How did you feel in the dream?" or "What seemed most important to you in the dream?" He might have responded to our query by saying that he felt as if wrong information were being pushed off on him and that what seemed most important was his certainty that the original route was best.

All of this is not to say that the feelings and responses of the dreamer are superfluous to dream interpretation. On the contrary, we can often arrive at valuable insights into our own attitudes and emotions by evaluating our dream responses. However, we must be careful not to stop at that point. We must realize that the dreamer is not infallible in his judgments and reactions to what is being presented as the events and symbols of the dream.

Another basic fact of dream interpretation is the possibility of multiple meaning for an individual dream. Once again drawing an analogy with mathematics, we note that certain equations can have multiple solutions. A simple example is $X^2=4$, in which X can equal either 2 or -2. Like a mathematical equation, a dream can occasionally be interpreted at several levels of meaning, each with its own validity and applicability. The following example from the readings illustrates this.

Q-1. . . .I was in bed and beheld a beautiful golden-haired child. Somebody else was viewing the child with me. "O, what a wonderful son to have," I said. "What a beautiful and ideal child. I surely wish God would give me one like that. I want a child." The child climbed into the other person's arms. "Other children are so different," I continued, "so lacking in these wonderful qualities. What a beautiful boy!" Then I beheld and heard the voice, both together. Voice: "You will have one child-son." I saw a tall young man, my own son, and he was eating at the table. He was attending college at this age. Voice: "He will be bright, very good in his studies and at college, but will be inclined to be wild. Might get into mischief."

A-1. In this there is presented to the entity, in this emblematical way and manner, a twofold lesson: for, as there is seen in this vision. . .this shall come to pass, for the entity will, in the flesh, have a son. [Baby son, [142], was born on 4/4/27.]

In the second. . .the sonship of self toward the higher forces is also represented, in the way and manner as the self may present itself for service.   **900-226**

*Q-2. . . .I entered a classroom with many students and I saw
written on the blackboard: "It is well for man to study the
three-tracked hobby horse that a child rides upon." I saw such
a hobby horse with its two rockers and an in-between wheel
that seemed like a bicycle wheel. I did not seem to understand
the significance.*

A-1. In this we find that the lesson is presented to the entity
in the threefold manner, through these conditions as are
presented in the emblematical way and manner—that
childhood first should be studied, and that the hobby of each
and every individual is the developing of the individual to the
highest points—for, as is seen, the hobby of an individual is as
the working of the inner man—as the inner wheel.

Again there is seen the warning to the entity that the entity
should beware of the hobby horse of this character in the
home, unless prepared by entity itself—for through the
construction of such a one as seen by entity much monies might
be made, see?

Then we have the spiritual, the physical, the financial, as
presented to the entity, and each should be studied by the
entity. Do that.   900-303

In working with our own dreams it will be important to keep
in mind this multiple-interpretation possibility. Our conscious
thinking tends to be rather linear—that is, we attempt to find
the solution to a given problem. For example, if X+4=6, then X
can equal only 2. In daily life, when we encounter multiple, and
seemingly contradictory, solutions to a problem, our tendency
may be to feel frustrated. However, dream experience is not
identical to waking experience. A dream comes from a level of
our being for which paradox and multiple meanings are quite
natural.

In the two excerpts from the readings just cited, the multiple
meanings do not seem to be contradictory. That is, we do not
find it hard to accept one without rejecting another. In the first
dream there is a precognitive statement of a coming male child,
as well as a lesson concerning the dreamer's own sonship with
the Divine. In the second dream there are three messages: (1) a
pun on the word "hobby" suggesting the spiritual necessity of
working on the inner self, (2) a warning not to have an actual
hobby horse in the home, presumably related to safety reasons,
and (3) the possibility of financial gain by constructing and
marketing hobby horses.

However, what if we should find two interpretations for a
particular dream which seem to contradict each other? This
must especially be considered if we are trying to use a dream to
make a decision for us. One psychologist, experienced with a
spiritual approach to dream study, has had many people share
with him dreams which they felt were giving explicit

instructions for some course of action. He has noted that for virtually every one of those dreams he could see alternative interpretations which suggested the opposite course of action. Such a concept may appear rather discouraging to those who hope to find a source of guidance through dreams. However, if we examine things more closely we see that this causes a problem for us only if we expect dreams to tell us what to do or make our choices for us. Rather, we can approach guidance more from the perspective that a dream frequently gives us feedback on our conscious decisions. If that feedback is ambiguous it simply means that we may have to take into consideration some opposing points of view before arriving at a final decision.

As an illustration of this point, consider the following hypothetical dream. Imagine that a young man has been contemplating alternatives in his relationship with his girlfriend. He dreams that they are getting married, but in the dream he is late for the wedding because he forgot it was his wedding day. Since the dream depicts a wedding, is this guidance suggesting marriage? Does it indicate that if he tries to pursue a marriage something will go wrong? Or does it show that he has some unconscious fear or resistance to marrying this person that might make him want to forget his wedding day? If the dreamer expects the dream to make his decision for him, then all these possible meanings create problem. However, if he simply uses the dream as a source of feedback on his conscious thoughts, then all the possible interpretations become important questions that he should answer for himself.

A final basic principle of interpretation concerns series of dreams which may contain the same message or lesson. Many people have found that working with a single dream is quite difficult and that only when they examine a series of their own dreams do the meanings become clear. The dreams in such a series may be all from the same night or from successive nights. Occasionally we may even find it useful to work with a set of dreams that are separated from each other by weeks or months.

If we remember several dreams each night we may wonder how to separate or categorize them into meaningful sets. One method is to look for recurrent symbols. For example, one might identify a series of dreams in which large bodies of water play an important role. Or one might find a series of dreams which all have a similar setting, such as one's childhood home. Such methods do not guarantee that each dream in the series has an identical meaning, but they do provide a broader perspective than working with just a single dream. In other words, a *set* of dreams with a recurrent symbol makes it more likely that one can catch the subtlety of meaning within that symbol. A set of dreams with a recurrent symbol makes it more likely that one can catch the subtlety of meaning within that symbol. A set of dreams from a given night can be especially valuable if a single problem or overriding concern has occupied the mind during the period of sleep and dreaming.

Cayce's dream interpretations frequently referred to a recurrent message in series of dreams. In the following instance, a pair of dreams from the same night indicates a need for the dreamer to accept help from others, especially his wife.

Q-2. ...Was standing in a rowboat and my wife was pulling me in to land. Then they seemed to be carrying her under a shed...

A-2. This [is] a presentation of the recognition of help and assistance that may be given the individual through the efforts of this body, [the wife]...

Q-3. Saw the house on the ocean drive I am thinking of taking for next summer in Deal. The words: "let [your wife] attend to that." Then thought of some house some one man was building. I wondered at his attempting to build this house alone. No one else was doing it. Maybe the words "Let [136] attend to that." came here instead of above—not sure.

A-3. This, as we see, again a representation to the individual of how self is attempting to build the self, the house of the mind of the individual. . .The words "Let [136] attend to that" coming, then, as the warning that the individual should consider the aid that may be had through others, rather than acquiring all through self.   900-98

Summary

Dream interpretation is far more than just the translation of symbols. The message or lesson of a dream, depicted in symbols, must maintain its living, meaningful nature. The real interpretation comes in applying the dream in daily life. Clearly, only the dreamer can make that application, and hence he is the best interpreter of his own dream. Furthermore, the very process of working (and playing!) with a dream is of great value to self-understanding and growth in consciousness. Even if we do not feel we have solved a dream, the very act of writing it down in a journal and attempting to interpret it provides growth in awareness about ourselves and the world around us.

In working with a dream there are two key factors we should consider: the dreamer (i.e., his responses and feelings in the dream) and the dream (i.e., the events and symbols). Interpretation of a particular dream should not limit itself to just one of these factors, nor should these two be confused. We must be especially alert to possible multiple meanings as we work with the symbols of a dream. Examining series of dreams is an effective aid for choosing among alternative possible interpretations.

Exercise in Application

Work with several of your own dream symbols from the various perspectives that have been suggested. If possible, select a symbol that appears in more than one of the dreams you have recorded. It can be a dream character, an animal or an inanimate thing.

First look at the dream (or preferably the series of dreams) as if that symbol literally represents itself in waking life. If this were the case, what would the dreams be showing you about this person or this thing?

Then look at the symbol as if it represents a part of your own personality (maybe a part you have not recognized or do not want to look at!). To help you see the symbol from this perspective, first write down the associations you have with that character, animal or thing. What qualities does it have? In waking life, what are your attitudes and feelings toward it? Then see if any of these associations fit a part of yourself—perhaps even a part of yourself you do not express very often.

Finally, look at the symbol for the possibility of a pun or a play on words. Sometimes the pun will be evident only by considering the context in which the symbol is used or the action in which it is involved.

Do not be surprised if you find that more than one approach to this symbol seems to give you some measure of insight into the dream. However, if you do not get anywhere with the first symbol you work on, choose another one (again, preferably one that appears in more than one dream) and go through the same procedure.

Chapter Four
KNOWING OURSELVES THROUGH DREAMS

The ancient injunction to "know thyself" is especially appropriate to dream study. If we record, examine and apply our dreams we cannot help but come to a greater knowledge of ourselves. Such knowledge will pertain to every level of our being. We will know our bodies and their requirements for health; we will know our personalities and those patterns of thought and feeling that may need transformation; and we will know the image of wholeness and perfection that is written within our souls.

In this chapter we will explore two techniques for interpreting a dream. Both are primarily based on the concept of knowing ourselves. The first approach was developed largely by Fritz Perls and is referred to as Gestalt therapy dream work. It is a well-known technique and its value has been repeatedly demonstrated. Although Cayce never directly mentioned this approach, the basic principles upon which it is founded are contained in the readings. The second approach was developed independently by several dream theorists and has been termed in various manners. We can call it the thematic approach, and in this case there is ample evidence that Cayce employed the technique in helping dreamers toward greater self-knowledge.

Dream Elements as Part of Self

Some writers have suggested that everything that appears in every dream is simply a part of oneself. Because of the large number of dreams which Cayce interpreted in a rather literal fashion, we have to conclude that the readings do not completely support such a notion. It may be true that for every dream we can find *some* degree of validity in an interpretation that treats each symbol as a part of oneself. However, the question we seek to answer in dream study remains "What is the *best* way for me to understand this dream?" Cayce's answer would be that only sometimes is the best interpretation one that treats each element of the dream as an aspect of oneself. Such a qualification, however, should not be discouraging unless one insists on having a single method of interpretation that always works. Rather, we should examine this valuable technique and be willing to try it on almost every dream, remembering that it will not always lead to the best answer.

A few examples will show us when and how the readings use this approach. In the first passage the emphasis is upon the characters of the dream and the way in which they portray aspects of the dreamer's personality. In other words, the dreamer is meeting parts of himself. Through the process of dreaming these elements of the personality are objectified so that they can be encountered and understood more clearly. One character represents a consciousness of lack (the lean man) and the other represents a consciousness of supply (the stout man).

Q-5. *I transacted business with two men seated at desks— one a stout one, the other lean. The former did the talking and as we concluded our business, I said: "You may need Cayce and his work." "Well, if we do, we'll write him and send him a check," they remarked scathingly. "You have everything you want," they continued. "Well," I replied, for I didn't want to complain or ask for too much, "I do so want to build that hospital in Virginia Beach." They looked at each other. "Well," said the stout man, "get a mortgage and have it transferred up here." I didn't understand him.*

A-5. In this there is seen in this emblematical way and manner that presented to the entity which has troubled, and is troubling, the entity as regarding those endeavors in which the entity hopes to engage itself and to interest others in. As is seen, there is the lean side and the fat side, and the lean side is as the conversationalist, or the one presenting the pessimistic side of those conditions as the entity hopes to and does engage self in. . .for the entity has that which it needs; yet there is felt within self that there is something lacking. . .Then, as is seen . . . procure a mortgage on same and transfer same here. . .

900-318

In the second and third examples the focus is upon both the character, which represents a part of the dreamer's personality, and the activity in which he is engaged. In other words, an important clue as to what aspect of self is being depicted rests with the description of what that character is doing. In these examples the actions are fishing (i.e., searching for something) and leading others.

Q-1. *A tall, thin man was in a sitting position, holding my silver-handled cane in his hand. He was using the cane as a fishing pole. The man's expression was very peculiar.*

A-1. In this we see an emblematical condition that presents the attitude of the individual self at the present time. And the attitude and expression of the individual seen is as that of the self in attempting to gather, to attain, something in the silver from the sources as are being studied by the entity.   137-24

Q-5. *Just what type of experience was that which I saw in a dream of several years ago of a tall light-headed man in a red cape leading a crowd up a hill near ... N.C., about Aug. 1, 1935?*
A-5. That was of self, or the ability of seeing self directing that which was and is a portion of the entity's experiences. Learn the lessons from these. In each and every one of thine experiences, as has been indicated, there are the basic truths and purposes and tenets from which lessons may be gained. Have the courage to give these to others!   853-9

In the final example which follows, the emphasis is primarily upon the process or activity depicted in the dream. Certainly, in this dream, the boy represents the dreamer; however, the focus of Cayce's interpretation was upon the process of "being run over." The warning is that the dreamer should beware of being run over by self, presumably through stress or neglect of the physical body.

Q-8. *Saw a boy run over by an automobile.*
A-8. ... the body viewing *self,* see? Then, *don't get run over* by self, so that it brings into the physical conditions of the body that which to the physical is being represented by an individual being run over! No reference to an individual, save to self.   137-54

As we explore the thematic approach we will see more clearly how the process or action shown in the dream may relate primarily to what is going on within the dreamer himself. The Gestalt technique, however, centers less on the process of the dream and more on the actual characters and symbols—that is, the *form* the dream takes. We have just seen supportive evidence from the readings that the form of the dream may simply represent parts of oneself. Now let us examine specific steps for applying that concept.

Gestalt Techniques

A character or object in a dream may represent a part of ourselves that has been forgotten, misunderstood or rejected. In this sense, we can say that there are patterns of energy within our being that are disassociated or broken off from our conscious selves. In order to integrate these parts of ourselves, in order to be whole, we must reclaim and reunite the elements that are in some way alienated. Since dreams may frequently show us such aspects, a very direct way to start this integrating process is to *identify ourselves* with such symbols. In other words, one can begin to reclaim misunderstood or unknown parts of oneself by consciously bringing self-awareness to them.

The Gestalt technique is to role play the given symbols and characters of a dream. On the one hand, this permits the traits we associate with that symbol to flow freely to mind. For example, if I role play the dream symbol of a tiger, pretending momentarily that I am a tiger, I may discover that I associate aggressive power with this animal. Role playing is usually a more powerful technique than the rather detached questioning which merely asks "What does this symbol remind me of?" A deeper understanding can take place when we identify ourselves with something else. We all know this from the experience of feeling greater empathy for someone who has a problem similar to one we have had. And so, in our example, the Gestalt approach would lead us to say, *"I am* a tiger. I feel...and I think ... "

Not only will such a technique increase the flow of associations with a symbol, but it also initiates the communication process between the conscious and unconscious elements of self. Upon role playing a symbol, an individual frequently discovers that there may be much more to its meaning than appears on the surface. By playing the role of a tiger, one may discover that the tiger also has a gentle, loving quality. It may feel misunderstood because it is always seen as aggressive and ruthless. We might well imagine such a situation within the personality of an individual, and the dream could simply be pointing out the need for self-knowledge regarding this condition.

Anyone who works with such role-playing techniques quickly discovers a fact that is both exciting and disturbing. In role playing one is likely to step well beyond the content of the dream itself, exploring deep into forgotten or hidden feelings. The dream can then become merely a jumping-off point for a deeper kind of analysis. It may be used as no more than a stimulus for a projective exercise, similar to showing someone an inkblot and asking him what he sees and how he feels toward it. In other words, if deeply pursued, the Gestalt technique moves well beyond simply working with a dream into a profound kind of psychotherapy.

If the reader wishes to explore Gestalt dream work seriously, it is strongly recommended that he find a professional who has had training with such an approach. There are many amateur

Gestalt therapists, primarily because the tools are easy to learn. But however easy it may be to use the role playing of dream symbols to achieve an entry into the unconscious, it is *not* easy to guide another person skillfully to an integration of all the elements of the unconscious that may be awakened. It is far easier to stimulate the awareness of a hidden part of the self than it is to bring that part into integration and wholeness with the rest of the personality.

Despite these warnings, among the tools of the Gestalt therapist there are some very simple and effective steps that the layman can use. They can be carried out on one's own or with a friend, provided that the friend agrees not to push the process should it become uncomfortable. The first step is to relate the dream—to oneself or to the friend—in the present tense. For example, one would say, "I *am* walking alone along the beach," rather than, "I *was* walking alone along the beach." One purpose for doing this is to emphasize the fact that the dream may depict a condition that currently exists in the dreamer, not just something that happened while he was sleeping last night.

The next step is to select the key symbols of the dream—usually two or three. They may be the key characters and objects in the dream, or the dreamer may use his intuition to choose a seemingly minor symbol which might have a deeper importance. The dreamer then goes through a multistage process (described below) with each of these key symbols, dealing with them one by one. In every stage he should speak in the first person—that is, using the pronouns "I" and "me"—and in the present tense. Some or all of the following questions can be answered. If the dreamer is working with a helper, that person can ask the questions.

1. How would you describe yourself? This is an opportunity for the dreamer to make an initial identification with the dream character or object (e.g., "I am a piano, a rather large one, and black in color"). The answer to this question will typically take from one-half to three minutes. Often when one simply gets "inside" the symbol in this way, an understanding will come concerning its meaning.

2. How do you feel? Now we are asking the dreamer to move from an intellectual function to the emotional content of the symbol. Some individuals may have trouble distinguishing between what they think and what they feel. Here is where the helper may be very useful, gently reminding the dreamer when he makes a statement that reflects what he thinks about something rather than what he is feeling. As was mentioned previously, at this point in the Gestalt process we may begin to move beyond what was happening in the dream. If the purpose of the investigation is purely self-exploration, associations and

feelings may be entertained as they come to mind. However, if the purpose is specifically to work on a particular dream, it is best to limit statements to how that symbol might be feeling, as the dream unfolds.

3. What do you want? Many symbols represent an unfulfilled part of the self. As the dreamer role plays a symbol and answers this question, he may gain an insight into an area of his life that needs more attention or completion.

4. What might you say to the other key symbols in the dream? It has been said that communication is often the first step toward healing. This applies not only to interpersonal relations, but also to the healing of the internal parts of ourselves. Sometimes the symbols in our dreams may represent elements of ourselves that are not working together, that are not integrated. It is a movement toward wholeness to initiate dialogue between these parts. In the dialogue between dream characters, the dreamer plays the various roles in alternating fashion. Usually it is helpful to have separate chairs for each character, the dreamer moving to the respective seat when each symbol chooses to speak. A trained Gestalt therapist can be especially useful in this stage.

In the following example we observe the first three of these stages being completed. In this instance the meaning of the dream became evident by the third step. The dreamer was not familiar with Gestalt techniques, and a helper asked the questions. If the dreamer had been acquainted with these steps, she probably could have completed this process on her own. This account is presented in abbreviated form in order to highlight the progress through the three stages.

Helper: Will you please tell the dream in the present tense.

Dreamer: Well, it was pretty short. I dreamed I saw a guitar, and . . .

H: Wait—in the present tense, okay? So you would say, "I see a guitar . . . "

D: I see a guitar and, well, all I can remember is that this guitar has a missing middle string.

H: Well, there's only that one symbol, but let's work with it. Could you be that guitar and tell me about yourself?

D: Let's see, it was a normal looking guitar . . .

H: I am a normal looking guitar . . .

D: Oh, yes. And I am about three feet long with only five strings—my middle one is missing. I am light brown in color and made of wood.

H: Anything else?

D: No, that's about it.

H: Tell me how you feel.

D: Well, I feel that I don't look too nice with that string missing.

H: That's what you think. What do you feel?

D: I feel a bit inadequate—somewhat incomplete. I guess I feel frustrated, too.

H: What do you want?

D: I want to have that missing middle string back.

H: What would it be like if what you want came true?

D: Well, then the chords, the music, played on me would be much more rich and full.

At this point in working with the dream there was a rather emotional moment for the dreamer as an insight dawned as to what the dream might mean. She related shortly thereafter that she suddenly saw that she had been talking about her own life. The missing middle string was that missing inner life—her recent failure to take time for personal meditation and self-reflection. If she were to regain this missing part of her life, the promise of a rich experience in all that she did could be fulfilled.

This example is especially noteworthy in that it points out how the role-playing technique can be effective with even a fragmentary dream. Quite probably, her dream experience had been much more lengthy than the small portion she recalled. Nevertheless, this technique proved useful with a single symbol, and a greater degree of self-knowledge was attained.

In summary, the technique of role playing the symbols of a dream is based on the concept that everything depicted in the dream may be an aspect of oneself. By directly identifying with these symbols and the energy of our own personality they represent, we can come to know ourselves more completely.

Knowing Self Through Life Themes

When we consider the term "self-knowledge" we may think first of the various facts we know about ourselves. Those facts can relate to the physical self, such as our height, weight, hair color and so forth. Or they can concern the personality, such as the things we fear or how we are likely to respond in a given situation. The facts can even be spiritual ones, describing the nature of our relationship with the Divine. However, such self-knowledge is rather static. It describes conditions as they are, without necessarily appreciating either the changing, unfolding nature of things or the way in which the facts may influence each other.

Such shortcomings suggest a further kind of self-knowledge—one which examines the dynamic, interactive part of life. We can know and understand ourselves by exploring the *processes* that are going on around us. The distinction between process and form is a vital one if we are to comprehend the spiritual dimension of life and of dreams. An analogy is often effective to explain that difference. Consider the nations of the world as forms or as structures. If we would study those nations in an academic way our tendency might be to learn the facts about each one: its population, geography, climate, etc. However, even if we were to learn those details for every country of the world, we would not really understand how the world operates. Our study would have to include the way in which the nations interact (through trade, treaties, competition, etc.) and how the process of that interaction changes the nature of each country. This analogy is especially pertinent to dream study. If we let the nations of the world represent the symbols of a particular dream, we see that we do not achieve a full understanding of the dream simply by learning all the facts about the individual symbols. That is, the potential a dream offers for self-knowledge is not limited to an exploration of the symbology.

There is a process going on in nearly every dream, and it is simply the way in which the characters and other symbols are interacting with each other. Certainly it is a major step toward self-understanding to recognize that those symbols may represent facts about ourselves. We see this every time we study a dream and exclaim, "My gosh, that dream character really is just like a part of me!" However, it is an equally important, though admittedly more subtle, step toward self-understanding to recognize oneself in the *process* of what is happening in the dream. This amounts to being able to say, "The way those dream characters and symbols are interacting is just like a part of my daily life." Such a recognition is the essence of the thematic approach to dream interpretation.

The basics of the thematic approach are really quite simple. We try to find a one-sentence summation of what is going on in the dream. If the dream is very long or has several scenes it may be best to break it apart temporarily and develop a thematic statement for each portion. Some people find the following analogy helpful to understand exactly what a theme means. Most television programming magazines have a brief description of each show. The purpose of that description, which often consists of just one sentence, is to summarize the essence of the program. There are some slight differences between a television synopsis and a dream theme, but there is an essential similarity: each says in as few words as possible what is going on.

Some dreams have an obvious and brief theme. For example,

"I am running away from something" or "I am caught in a frustrating situation" are frequent dream themes for many of us. In other cases it is more difficult to extract the essential process taking place. With consistent practice, however, a dreamer can become quite adept at restating his dream in thematic terms which may reveal its meaning. Before examining the steps involved in determining a dream theme, we should explore just how a theme can unlock the dream's message.

How the Dream Theme Works

The fundamental principle of the thematic approach is that our daily lives are made up of identifiable types of interaction and unfoldment. In other words, there are the processes that are going on in each person's life that give it a changing, growing character. The interactions are often with other people, and each has a quality and a pattern to it; for example, a relationship with another may have a quality that includes attempted openness and honesty, but also the problems caused by the withholding of certain things. In other cases the interactions are among parts of ourselves; for instance, a person experiences such a relationship when he treats his body thoughtlessly and consequently falls into mental depression. We can think of our lives as being made up of a collection of patterns or themes of experience that characterize our interactions.

The hypothesis underlying the thematic approach to dream work is that our dream experiences reflect the basic patterns of daily life. This reflection may take the form of guidance, a warning, or simply a depiction of things as they are. The meaning or message of a dream may be a commentary on a particular theme being carried out in daily life. The commentary is sometimes contained in the symbology of the dream, although frequently the meaning of the dream is simply to *call attention* to the fact that a particular pattern of experience is going on in waking life.

The procedure for using the theme of a dream as an interpretation tool can best be explained by an illustration. In the diagram below, the contents of daily life experience are represented by various shapes—that is, patterns of behavior, of thinking and of feeling. In using the theme approach we try to identify the basic, overall "shape" of the dream, and then we look for the areas of waking life that it matches.

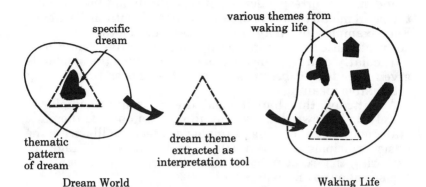

specific dream

various themes from waking life

thematic pattern of dream

dream theme extracted as interpretation tool

Dream World

Waking Life

Once we discover an area of daily life that the theme matches, we are much more likely to be able to interpret properly the symbols contained in that dream. Occasionally we may not need to go back to the symbols because the meaning may simply be to call attention to the theme's applicability to daily life. However, when we do need to return to the symbology to extract a meaning, we have taken an important step forward: we have discovered the likely *context* in which the symbol is being used. Since many symbols have several possible interpretations, the knowledge of the context is extremely valuable.

As an example of how things might work, consider the following hypothetical dream. "I am being chased at night down the deserted streets of a city. My pursuer seems to be an animal, maybe a lion. I am extremely frightened. At one point in my running I notice my mother standing at a street corner about a block away." The dreamer will encounter problems if he begins work on this dream by listing the symbols and attempting to determine the meaning of each one. In the case of the mother there are several possible meanings; that symbol could represent the actual mother, a quality of the mother which is also in the dreamer, or the archetype of the Great Mother. Simply to make a guess from among these choices is likely to result in the wrong selection.

Using the theme approach will be especially helpful in this case. A simple theme for this dream would be "I am running away from something." The next step is for the dreamer to look for areas of his waking life in which that theme may match a life condition. Several matches may be found, but in this case let us suppose he finds only one: he has been running away from a confrontation with a fellow employee at work. He has been harboring some resentments and anger but has avoided a face-to-face discussion of the situation with the person. Having found such a correspondence between the dream theme and a theme from daily life, the dreamer can work with the symbols. For example, he may recall that his mother has the characteristic of suppressing her negative emotions, particularly of never showing her anger. Once the symbol is given a context, it becomes far easier to choose from among alternative meanings.

Admittedly, this hypothetical dream is quite simplistic. Rarely do our own dreams contain such an obvious thematic statement. However, this example does serve to illustrate the basic principles of this method, and it sets the stage for exploring the exact procedure for discovering and using the themes of our own dreams.

Steps in Finding the Theme

As previously mentioned, the first step in formulating an effective theme for a particular dream is to make sure you have a workable piece of material. If the dream is only a fragment, such as the guitar dream described earlier, this approach simply is not going to work. On the other hand, if the dream is unwieldy and has many scenes, consider working with it in parts. One may later find that the parts of the dream fit together better than expected. However, one should not be too quick to divide the dream into sections merely because it is long. A person skilled at the thematic approach can see through all the rambling events to the heart of what is happening in the dream story.

The second step is to identify the key action words of the dream as it is recorded in the dream journal. Here we are looking for the *verbs*. They will tend to be much more important to this process-oriented theme than the nouns (i.e., the symbols) will be. This is not to say that the nouns are unimportant, but rather that the theme is concerned with the movement and interaction of the dream events. We have already seen in our examination of symbology that we have a problem with some symbols in that they have multiple possible meanings. The theme may help us with this dilemma by identifying the context in which the symbol is being used. In this sense, *the thematic technique is a preliminary step* to interpretation. In using it we are trying to do some groundwork that will allow us to interpret the dream more effectively. So, as one works on writing a dream theme he must be patient. He must temporarily ignore the symbols (i.e., the nouns), even though they may look pregnant with meaning, and focus on the verbs and important adjectives and adverbs.

Once we have selected the key action words of the dream, the third step is to do something with the nouns which are linked to those actions. For example, if I choose "running away" as a key action phrase of the dream, obviously some dream character was performing that action. This step involves "generalizing" those nouns. This means making them more fuzzy and less specific. A specific person can be replaced with the word "someone"; a particular object can become "things" or "something." Combining these words with our action phrase, we might come up with the theme "Someone is running away from something."

In actually formulating the theme one should not hesitate to make it short. Frequently a theme of only four or five words will work quite well. If an initial, short theme fails to unlock the meaning of the dream, then the dreamer can go back and lengthen the thematic statement so as to include other key words or actions from the dream.

It should be noted as well that more than one theme can be possible for a particular dream. We can view any experience from a variety of perspectives. Just as two people can watch the same event and see it differently, we should learn to observe our dream experiences from alternative points of view. When Cayce seemed to be using the theme approach in dream readings, he had the advantage of psychic perception to know which of several possible themes would work best. In working with our own dreams, we often must try out several alternatives before finding that one which gives us the optimal aid for interpretation.

With any technique there should be clear instructions on what to do if the technique does not work. Two such courses of action have already been suggested for use with this method of dream work: making a short theme longer by incorporating more key words, and creating a new theme by taking a different perspective. Taking a different perspective is most easily done by merely focusing attention on a different portion of the dream.

Another procedure to try when the initial theme fails to match any aspect of waking life is to make the nouns less generalized. Recall that we have replaced the key characters and symbols with generalizing words like "someone" and "something." It may be necessary to back off from that extreme position. For example, we may have replaced the symbol of a schoolhouse with the words "some place." If our theme has not worked, we might want to try a term that is slightly more specific yet still leaves room for the possibility that the schoolhouse should not be taken literally. Perhaps the phrase "a place of learning" would be effective. This procedure may work for dream characters as well. One's sister in a dream may have initially been replaced with "someone." But if the initial theme has failed to unlock the dream, a better generalizing phrase might be "a woman closely related to me."

In summary, we should be willing to play with various alternatives for a dream theme. Although the action of the dream is usually most significant in formulating the theme, there are cases in which we must include certain general qualities of the symbols. If we establish too rigid a set of rules for creating dream themes, we destroy that playful, experimental attitude that is so necessary for this technique.

Applying Dream Themes for Interpretation

At a time just after he had been introduced to the dream-theme method, a young man had the following dream. This individual, in his mid-twenties, for many years had been using his dreams as a source of self-knowledge.

> I dreamed that I am walking along a strange road at night. I have several glass bottles in my hands and for some reason I throw them—one after another—onto the pavement of the road, where they shatter. Then I realize that I was foolish to do this because I will be driving along that very road tomorrow and will probably puncture a tire on a piece of the glass.

At this point the reader might want to cover up the rest of this page and make an attempt to write a theme for this dream. The guidelines proposed in the previous section should be useful steps to employ. In the case of the dreamer, on his first attempt he wrote, "I am breaking something." However, he could find no place in his daily life where that theme seemed appropriate. On his second attempt he focused on a slightly different aspect of the experience and wrote, "I am doing something that will cause trouble for me later." As he examined the areas of his waking life for correspondences to this theme, there seemed to be many possibilities; but the theme was not specific enough to permit a meaningful choice.

Going back to the dream, he selected one critical modifier that had been left out of the theme—there had been a quality of carelessness or thoughtlessness to his action. The third try at the theme proved successful: "I am thoughtlessly doing something that may cause trouble for me later." This pattern seemed to match what was going on in a relationship with a specific person. Recently he had had a very critical attitude toward that person and was verbally sharing his complaints with others. Through this dream he realized that he was probably creating further difficulties with his actions, problems that he would have to meet later.

Of course, it is hard to say whether or not that was in fact the proper meaning of the dream. Assuming that the dreamer subsequently *acted* on his insight, he had found an interpretation which seemed useful to him. We do not have a psychic source to validate our use of this dream theme as we do with the Cayce dream readings, but the fact that a practical application was discovered demonstrates the effectiveness of the thematic technique.

The present writer has frequently used this particular dream as an example for workshop purposes. It seems to be an especially good one for participants to try as an exercise in learning to write a theme. However, anywhere from twenty to eighty percent of the group members typically fail to write a dream theme, but rather write what they feel the dream means. Frequent answers include "The dreamer isn't eating well," and "What you sow, so shall you reap." It is possible that these answers could be a type of interpretation, but they are certainly *not* dream themes. The theme should limit itself to *what is found in the dream itself.* In this particular dream there are no references to eating, sowing or reaping. Because this kind of jumping to conclusions happens so often in dream-theme workshops, it is probably wise for the reader to pay special attention to this pitfall. Do not get ahead of yourself; the dream theme is usually a preliminary step to interpretation, and formulating it requires that you limit yourself to that which is specifically in the dream itself.

Dream Themes in the Cayce Readings

The dream readings appear to be full of examples in which the thematic approach is used. In some of the interpretations Cayce also examines the symbols, but they are given their context by the theme. In other cases it is the theme itself that is the heart of the dream message. The following five excerpts are good examples of how a theme can unlock the dream's meaning. The reader may wish to read the respective dream, make an effort to write down the theme as he sees it, and then read Cayce's interpretation. In brackets after each interpretation will be found one way of expressing the theme which the readings seem to have identified, and a statement of where the theme was applicable in the dreamer's life.

Q-5. Night of July 19 or Tuesday morning July 20, I seemed to be going to play golf with Edwin Weisel and [my wife]. They started—took their first shot when I discovered I had left my clubs in the locker and must go after them. It would be too late upon returning to play with them, for they couldn't hold people up waiting for me. I was sorry, for I didn't like [my wife] alone in this company.

A-5. Again an emblematical condition as is presented to the entity, as to the preparedness for the various phases of any condition in which the entity would enter. . .   900-252

["Things go wrong because I wasn't prepared"; generally applicable to every aspect of the dreamer's life.]

Q-2. I was going in bathing in the ocean surf and started to dive into a breaker, but instead found that I dived headfirst right into the sand and was caught there headfirst. [My wife] called to [4167] to help and they tried to pull me out. I woke up trying to breathe, but was having great difficulty and feeling that I was suffocating from my experience in the sand.

A-2. As is seen, the ocean represents that as to which all life in the material or physical plane proceeds, in its way and manner. The sand is the basis of the thing. Diving headfirst, then, into, as it were, the ocean of experience, the entity may find self fast in same. . .

. . .the lessons are then as steppingstones, and *wade* in, rather than dive in headfirst. For little by little, line upon line, line upon line, must one gain the full concept of the conditions in which one lives, moves, and has its being.   137-84

["Diving headfirst into something gets me into difficulty"; applicable to the way the dreamer tends to approach a new condition.]

Q-7. I was sick—worn down—nervous, and my lungs were affected. I was being examined (they took my temperature and found I had fever), and they told me I would have to go away— to Saranac. I was partially undressed and in an office with a window open, as I am when I take an osteopath treatment. The doctor sitting behind a desk, said: "You should not sit like that in front of an open window." "If only [137] would take a vacation—he needs one—then I would take one. We both need a rest away from work," I said. "Yes," agreed the doctor. "That would help me, a trip to Havana or something of the kind." They were worried about my lungs.

A-7. This, as we see, referring rather to the mental condition of the entity, as its relation to the stock market, rather than to physical conditions of the body. . .the entity should then *clear out* of the market until there is some settled condition in same...   900-271

["Unstable conditions mean I need to get away for a while"; applicable to the instability of the stock market and advisability of getting out.]

Q-6. Went into store and asked for 10¢ worth of jelly beans and they handed me just 4 beans. "Is that all I get for 10¢?" I asked. They told me just 4. "Well, then, how much are chocolates?" I asked, thinking to buy them instead of the beans. "Three for $1.00," came the reply. "Just 3?" I asked. "Three," came the reply. "Then you can keep your chocolates, too," I flatly stated and walked out.

A-6. This shows to the entity the inconsistency at times in self, as regards the various conditions that arise in the daily life, if the entity would but take the time to consider same from every viewpoint. For, as inconsistent as the prices are asked of entity, as inconsistent do many actions of self appear to others.

["Things which are inconsistent and unfair are being demanded"; applicable to the way the dreamer tends to treat others.]

Q-2. I saw my father. He was seated in a sort of tomb on an open iron grate. He did not seem so well. This place seemed connected with that Sunday School. I left my father to attend to some matters and when I returned to him, found he had died and fallen down into a dark pit of the tomb. I called to some of the higher-ups in the tomb (was terribly sorry—grieved) and said: "When did he take a turn for the worse?" "He fainted from weakness a little while ago, while you were gone," they called back to me, "and falling on the grates, rolling and fell down here." "Is he dead?" I called. "Not quite," they replied.

A-2. . . . In the leaving of same we find this presenting to the entity that which may occur to the entity by deferring the studies, the way in which would be gained the greater truths, so that by returning to same, after having given time to other things, there would be found the weakness and the falling away, the inability, as it were, of the help to come to the entity in the proper manner.   900-143

["I leave something but find on my return that things have gone badly"; applicable to unfavorable circumstances that will occur if the dreamer leaves off his studies.]

Some variations of this thematic approach are also found in the readings. In one instance (900-99, Q-4) the readings use a thematic statement of the *setting* of the dream to uncover its meaning. The dreamer finds himself sitting on the steps outside a university. Someone else comes out of the building talking about how his hair has turned white, yet he is really quite youthful. Cayce picked up on the notion of the dreamer being "outside the university" and indicated this was a theme pertinent to the dreamer's daily life. What was needed was application of what had already been learned, not more formal education at that time.

Another variation of the thematic approach involves using the nouns as if they were rather literal. A good example of this procedure is found in the following dream (195-33, Q-2). The dreamer is approached by a friend and asked for an empty bottle. Not having one, the dreamer goes to the basement in search of one. He finds an old one and starts to pick it up, only to find a large amount of paper money that belongs to no one. Clearly a good theme for this dream, if we retain the key symbols, would be "I am finding money with bottles." Cayce's interpretation was just that: a considerable sum of money can be made from a coming business venture that involves something which is bottled.

Other variations of the thematic approach are possible. The reader is encouraged to experiment with this method because it has proven to be a powerful tool for many people. The assumption on which it rests is quite sound: treat the dream first as a whole before examining the pieces.

Skill at this method will come with practice. It is easy to compare notes with others as you sharpen your skills at catching the essence of each dream. The dream-theme technique is especially good for group work. By pooling various points of view many alternative themes often can be developed for a single dream. The dreamer can then choose the one that seems most appropriate. An added benefit is that in helping another person formulate a theme for his dream you are not interpreting it for him. You are dealing strictly with the manifest content of the dream and not placing your own biases upon the translation of particular symbols. For those who wish further practice in writing dream themes, Appendix B contains more cases from the readings. Once again you can match your skill with that of Edgar Cayce in the psychic state.

Summary

Probably the most important purpose of dream study is self-knowledge. The dream is the direct product of that self we would understand. Certainly there may be instances in which dreams show us facts about others or about the future. However, to understand even those types of dreams we must actually know ourselves first. For this reason, we have begun our survey of dream interpretation techniques with two that focus on finding ourselves in the characters, symbols and events of the dream.

In one instance we have explored how each element of a dream may represent a part of the dreamer. Those parts are likely to be unknown or misunderstood ones. In this sense, they are part of ourselves that are cut off and require an integration with the whole. Gestalt-therapy role playing can be effective because it potentially initiates this healing process and because it stimulates a freer flow of associations with each dream symbol.

The second technique—the theme approach—promotes another variety of self-knowledge. By examining a dream as a whole, rather than in parts through its symbols, we can identify the significant patterns or processes that make up waking life. And such a step in dream study has the added benefit of accurately assessing the context in which the various symbols are used.

Exercise in Application

Work on a single dream with a group of people. Since there may be several possible themes contained within a single dream, make it a group effort to find more than one thematic perspective of the dream.

Then make an effort in your daily life to help someone understand one of his dreams. This should be a person other than the ones in your group. Do not try to interpret the dream for that person, but rather help to find its theme or themes. Allow that person to see if the theme fits daily life, but do not push the person any further in the interpretation than he or she is willing to go.

Chapter Five
IDEALS IN OUR DREAMS

Perhaps the most important concept found in the Edgar Cayce readings is the significant part of ideals in spiritual growth. We find the role of ideals emphasized in the readings on physical health, meditation, psychic development, reincarnation and a variety of other topics. Ideals are also a key to our understanding of Cayce's approach to interpreting dreams.

We can think of an ideal as a purpose or spirit of living. It is a fundamental consciousness toward life in general, and it forms the foundation of our daily thoughts, feelings and actions.

In the terminology of the readings, an ideal differs from a goal. The latter is more or less product-oriented; it focuses on the material outcome of our efforts. For example, one might have a goal of building a house by a certain date. It will become clear from a material point of view whether or not that goal was achieved. An ideal, however, is process-oriented, in that it concerns the spirit in which things are done. For example, it would relate to the attitudes and feelings with which one works on building that house. To help us get a better picture of what an ideal entails, some synonyms may be useful: motivation, purpose, values.

More accurately, we can talk about ideals at three levels: spiritual, mental and physical ideals. The spiritual ideal is actually the foundation upon which daily life is built. In order to determine our personal spiritual ideal, we might ask ourselves this question: "What is the overall spirit of living or feeling about life that I would like to have guiding and directing every aspect of my daily living?" This spirit or feeling is, of course, beyond words. It is a state of awareness. However, the Cayce readings encourage us to get a handle on the spiritual ideal by choosing a word or a short phrase that describes that awareness. Having a word or phrase is especially helpful during those times in which we may have drifted away from our ideal and want to get back in touch with it. The word or phrase acts as a tool or a reminder to reawaken the ideal spirit of living we have chosen. It becomes a type of personal "mantra" (meaning "mind tool"). Much has been made of the possession of a personal mantra to use in meditation. Certainly, when properly understood, the tradition of the mantra, which teaches that special chosen words have the capacity to transform consciousness, is a powerful one. Likewise, our spiritual ideal is represented by a carefully chosen word or phrase. It too can be used to change our consciousness in moments of confusion, simply by saying it aloud or silently to ourselves.

In selecting a word or short phrase to represent our personal spiritual ideal, we should not be too concerned about what others think our chosen words mean. In fact, only two things matter in our selection. First is that those words stimulate an awareness or a feeling in us that is worthy of being the guiding influence in all that we do. And, second is that the spiritual ideal genuinely be the one *by which we are willing to measure our lives.* Some of the words and phrases that have been chosen by individuals setting a spiritual ideal are kindness, peacefulness, compassion, universal love, and joyful service. We should write only something like "Christ Consciousness" if we are currently willing to measure our attitude and action by that standard.

It might be helpful to make a distinction between the spiritual ideal that we consciously select and the ideal of the spiritual forces within each soul. In the readings, the Bible and many other sources we find the principle that the human soul contains from its creation the image or pattern of the Divine. In the words of the readings, this is the Christ Consciousness—the awareness of our oneness with God, which is written like a pattern on the mind and is waiting to be brought into conscious awareness through the use of our will. This we might think of as the *Ideal,* and it is the same for everyone.

Our work in the earth is to become aware of that Ideal and manifest its qualities. A key step in that work is to determine our best understanding of the Ideal at the present time, and that step is the setting of a personal spiritual ideal. As we more closely adhere to the spirit of living described by our ideal, we come to a deeper understanding of the actual nature of the Ideal. Such a growth in awareness is likely to lead to a new concept of what our spiritual ideal should be. In other words, our spiritual ideal changes, reflecting our development in awareness as we approach that great Ideal within us all. We shall continue to use this distinction between an ideal and the Ideal throughout this chapter.

The process of unfoldment depends largely upon our capacity to adhere to the spiritual ideal we have most recently set. In order to do this, we are encouraged to set mental and physical ideals which correspond to our spiritual one. Our application of a spiritual ideal is through our mental attitudes and physical actions. Ideals at these two levels are therefore merely a reflection of what has been chosen as our single, overall spiritual focus.

For example, imagine that a woman selects the word "Healing" to represent her spiritual ideal. This means that she wishes to have every aspect of her life—at home, at work, in her times alone—guided by an influence of healing. And furthermore, she is willing to measure her life experiences by that ideal. In order to make it more likely that such a consciousness would direct her life, she would do well to express states of mind (i.e., attitudes) and behaviors that are in keeping with healing. Since most of our attitudes and actions are in *relationship to* conditions and people with whom we associate this is a good place to start. She might choose three significant people in her life and ask herself this question for each person: "What *attitudes* could I be holding in mind towards this individual which would be in keeping with a spirit of healing?" Perhaps for her relationship with her husband she would select the attitudes of "patience" and "appreciation." In other words, she realizes that as she holds these two attitudes in mind, her life is growing toward greater healing. Most likely, as she examines the other two relationships using the same question, she will determine ideal mental attitudes that are especially applicable to each of those unique relationships. Of course, mental ideals are not limited to our involvements with particular people. We can choose ideal attitudes toward groups of people, toward aspects of living—such as our job—and toward ourselves.

Equally important are our physical ideals. For each person, group or life situation for which we set mental ideals we should do the same with physical ideals. In our example, the woman would then ask herself this question in regard to each of the three significant people in her life: "What *actions* could I be *doing* in my relationship with this individual which would be in keeping with a spirit of healing?" Regarding her teenage son, with whom she has a tendency to bicker, she might write down the physical ideals of saying a prayer for him each morning and finding something complimentary to say to him each day.

In summary, mental and physical ideals are important because they direct us toward an application of the spiritual ideal we have set. There is probably a tendency in most all of us to set a lofty spiritual ideal and then fail to take steps toward realizing it. Such a tendency is not necessarily due to laziness. It may be that our spiritual ideal seems so far removed from our normal approach to life that we feel little hope of being able to live up to it very often. In such a case, the mental and physical ideals become like stepping-stones—they are the intermediary stages between where we are now and where we hope to be.

Ideals in the Creation of Dreams

A study of ideals is important not only to the proper interpretation of dreams, but also to an understanding of how they are created. In many ways, the one Ideal within us all plays a significant role in the production of dreams. First, the Ideal provides a particular influence or impetus to human experience. In a sense, the Ideal tends to lift us out of materiality and into another kind of experience: a deeper knowledge of the multidimensional nature of the soul. For most people this broadening of consciousness takes place most regularly in the dream life. We observed previously that dreams are God's method of providing a way of understanding for us. Another way of saying this is that the Ideal within us exerts a nightly influence to explore the inner world of the soul.

Of course, the influence and impetus of the Ideal is not only to lift us out of material existence. In a complementary fashion, it guides us to apply in material life that which has been revealed in higher-dimensional experience. This may in part explain Cayce's warning that dreams should not be viewed as a means of escape. That is, even though they give us a clue to the life beyond, they do not eliminate our responsibility to live lovingly in our daily affairs.

A second way in which the Ideal influences the creation of dreams concerns the correlation of forces. Recall that one of our definitions of a dream involves the correlation of spiritual, subconscious, mental and physical forces. In this case it is important to note that the term *force* has a special meaning: energy with a specific directional quality. That direction relates to ideals. For the spiritual forces, the direction is that path of spiritual unfoldment contained in the Ideal. For the other three types of forces, the direction relates to the conscious ideal held by an individual. Such an ideal may or may not correspond to the Ideal. For example, there are patterns of energy which relate to distant past experiences, and we call these patterns the subconscious forces. The memory of each such experience has a directional quality, which is the ideal that was being held in mind as the experience took place. Quite often that ideal was contrary to the divine Ideal within the soul. A similar state exists with regard to recent conscious thoughts (i.e., the mental forces) and the condition of the physical body (i.e., the physical forces).

We see, therefore, that both the Ideal and the various conscious ideals we have held in mind play an important role in dreams. Since a dream is produced by correlation of the forces, we can translate this to mean that dreams may be created by the interaction and comparison between ideals and the Ideal. Perhaps a less confusing way to say this would be that in our dreams there can be a weighing or a measuring of our material-world experiences versus the pattern of perfection written within the soul. In many of the readings we find this concept of a comparison creating a dream. Here are two examples:

Q-5. Are my dreams ever significant of spiritual awakening?
A-5. . . .In vision there is oft. . .an awakening between the mental consciousness, or that that has been turned over and over in the physical consciousness and mind being weighed with that the self holds as its ideal.   262-9

Sleep—that period when the soul takes stock of that it *has* acted upon during one rest period to another, making or drawing—as it were—the comparisons that make for Life itself in its *essence*. . .   5754-2

It may be only a rare dream in which the comparison between our attitudes and our ideals is literally depicted. Frequently the comparison is only implied or it is left to us to work in our interpretation. However, we may occasionally have a dream like the following example, in which the significance of ideals to dreams is boldly stated.

Q-8. I was back in a department store, a clerk behind the counter, even as I was in past days. I waited on people—serving them, but it seemed I was in love with some girl. Some dissatisfaction resulted and I was miserable. Then the Voice: "Here are you tested as much as anywheres." Then I felt terrible, as though I had failed in something, in living up to that which was expected of me—that I had retarded—returned to old conditions, instead of living the ideals I had set for myself.
A-8. Rather that in this as the interpretation and lesson: That often the self, mentally, spiritually, physically, should take stock of self, as is seen in department stores run on the correct basis, and that the loves for certain or for particular conditions that exist in the life, whether the mental or the desire of flesh, or the spiritual forces, all must be weighed well, and as the Voice is given, the test is that entity keeps the standard in that manner that gives the progressive forces to self and abilities to give out in service, as is necessary for advancement in every phase of the phenomenized life, see?
          900-156

There is a third way in which the Ideal influences the creation of dreams, one which concerns our recall of dream experiences. In regard to this, we should keep in mind that during sleep the soul has actual experiences. It is our conscious recall of them, usually brought back in symbolic form, that we label "a dream." The hypothesis we find in the readings (5754-3) is that our attunement to the Ideal is a major influence not only upon our ability to contact spiritual forces (e.g., through meditation), but also upon our capacity to retain the memory of our sleep experiences. In the sense that a dream is created by the quality of our memory of it, the Ideal once again is directly related to the formation of dreams.

Applying Ideals to Dream Interpretation

Among the various sources of theories about dreams, the Edgar Cayce readings are rather exceptional in their use of ideals in interpretation. Although a comparison involving the dreamer's ideals may not be required for the best interpretation of every dream, this perspective is one of the readings' major contributions. It, perhaps more than anything else, allows us to link dream study to spiritual unfoldment.

As an introduction to specific interpretation techniques using ideals, we would do well to consider a pair of principles which broadly relate ideals to working with our dreams. First, the readings suggest that the very purpose for dream study is development—not just any kind of development, however. Rather, the kind we are aiming for is that which leads us toward the higher forces, or the Ideal within us. Another way of saying this is that *the way to interpret a dream is to find how it leads you to a deeper experience of the Ideal.* The readings express it thus:

Q-44. How should dreams be interpreted?
A-44. ...Correlate those Truths that are enacted in each and every dream. . .and use such to the better developing, ever remembering [that] develop means going towards the higher forces, or the Creator.   3744-4

A second basic principle which relates ideals to interpretation concerns the nature of a symbolic dream image. A dream symbol can be understood to represent a *motivating force* within the dreamer—that is, an ideal. This is one of the most profound concepts in the Cayce dream readings. It was given in regard to the symbology of the Revelation of Saint John, but we can understand it to pertain to our own inner symbology as well. The passage in which this principle is stated is as follows:

> For the motivating force in each one of those patterns represented, is that which the individual entity entertains as the ideal. This is the motivating spirit, the motivating purpose. When it is out of attune, or not coordinating with the First Cause, there may not be the greater unfoldment.   4083-1

The reader is encouraged to consider this paragraph carefully. It is one of the most significant ones found in the Cayce material on symbols. It suggests that a dream shows us, through the variety of its symbols, the array of conscious ideals that we entertain in daily life. For example, an individual may experience in conscious life several types of motivating spirit or motivating purpose: to love and serve others, to attain material security, to be well liked by others, to take it easy and enjoy the pleasures of life. At different times of the day, that individual is likely to allow different motivations to guide him. In this sense, the individual has a variety of ideals and he vacillates among them. We can probably all identify with the person in this example to some degree. We may know that a particular ideal or motivating spirit is preferable to other ones, yet we may find it difficult to choose what is best for us.

Here is where our dreams can be especially helpful. A symbolic image may be thought of as representing a particular ideal that we occasionally entertain. The interactions that take place in our dreams can be seen as *the interactions between alternative ideals or spirits of living.* We can use the dream to identify those ideals that are most likely to be in attunement with the perfect Ideal within (i.e., "the First Cause").

This principle suggests our first specific method for using ideals in dream study. We can try to identify the patterns or images within a dream that seem to reflect our best ideals. Once we identify such dream symbols, we then observe the role they play in the dream events. This process is well illustrated in two examples from the readings.

In the first case, the dreamer (an 18-year-old man) reports dreaming that he and two companions were outdoors watching a dirigible and airship sailing above them. The dirigible ran into trouble and crashed to the ground. The dreamer heard the cries and groans of the occupants and started towards the wreck to help. However, the survivors warned him to stay back. In Cayce's interpretation of this dream (341-13, A-2) he identifies the airship and dirigible as "those high ideals as are held in the entity's mind." However, looking closer at the role that these symbolic representations play in the dream events, we see that they crash. Cayce points out that the ideals are without stability in the dreamer's life. A lack of "strength of character" is described as a weakness in the personality of the dreamer. We may presume that this characteristic results in a tendency to waver from those high ideals or in a failure to apply them. And so, in this example we see that the dream fulfills two functions. It depicts a significant motivating force in the dreamer's life, and it illustrates how the dreamer stands in relationship to that ideal.

In a second example from the readings, the person (a 31-year-old man) reports a dream in which he received a transfusion of his wife's blood. This was done in order to enrich his blood supply and furnish it with needed strength. In Cayce's interpretation of this dream (900-271, A-8) he identifies the blood as the "ideas and ideals of one individual." The blood seems to be an especially good representation of the life-giving quality of ideals. The role played by those ideals in the dream is one of transmission from one individual to another. The reading points out that the lesson of this dream is the value of sharing one's ideals and ideas with others. Greater strength and greater abilities (presumably for both the dreamer and whomever he shares his ideals with) are promised in Cayce's interpretation.

In these two examples we have seen that certain dream symbols can represent the high ideals of an individual and that the dream events provide a clue concerning the current role of such ideas. However, in some dreams, especially fragmentary ones, there may be little or no interaction between this key symbol and other parts of the dream. In such cases, our highest ideals may be represented in dreams simply to *remind us* that they exist.

For example, in reading 900-156, a 30-year-old man recalls this short dream: "Saw an old man—or one with iron gray hair walk by me." Cayce suggests that this was a symbol of the high ideal of understanding and knowledge. Such a quality existed within the dreamer and was merely being called to conscious awareness through the dream image. In a similar instance, a reading given for the same person recalls a forgotten dream of his, in which he saw a flagpole and a flag flying from it (900-69, A-3). Again, Cayce describes the portrayal of the high ideals within the dreamer—the standard by which he measures his life. We might suspect that the dream's primary purpose was to remind him that this standard did exist.

Occasionally our highest ideals are depicted in dreams not by a single symbol, but by the quality of the entire dream experience. These are the beautiful dreams that we occasionally have which remind us that there is a pattern of wholeness and joyful living within. A good example of this type is described in the following passage:

Q-1. [115]: After a group meditation for the folks in New York, I dreamed I was talking to and walking with Gladys. She said "They do not pay their rent." I asked who owned the place (we seemed near a house). Gladys said, "Mr. Cayce." The building seemed quite large and rambling and was at the Beach. We wandered around the place, and I noticed much iron rubbish, both old and new. Gladys seemed to fade out of the picture. I still wandered around the place, discovered a lovely lake, clear as crystal, beautiful white swans swimming around and being fed by loving happy children. Looking over the lake I saw there beautiful houses like a new settlement of beautiful happy homes, a white village, flowers, etc. Then I was so happy, felt uplifted, etc.

A-1. This, as is indicated, is emblematical of conditions within the development of the individual, or *entity*-individual itself, as to the individual ideal in that as is held in its consciousness.

...the visions of that as would *again* be held by the *entity*, or *individual*, as ideal, or idealistic, arise from the rubbish of those things material.   262-8

The first method of using ideals in dream study is based on the notion that our highest ideals are sometimes directly depicted in the images or overall quality of the dream experience; they come as *reminders*. A second method calls on us to *evaluate and compare* ideals. Such comparisons can be either of two varieties: (1) between alternative ideals illustrated in the dream, or (2) between an ideal depicted in the dream and the spiritual, mental or physical ideals we have consciously chosen.

The comparison of various ideals that are depicted in the dream can be made as we examine the symbols. Recall the concept that we can think of almost any symbol as a representation of some motivating force—that is, some ideal that we experience at least occasionally. Working with a dream in this manner may allow us to clarify which ideal from among several alternatives is the best one for us. Consider the following dream of a man, which simply illustrates this principle.

> I am working in my office on a special project that has been assigned to me. It is a challenging one—difficult, but one I know I can do well if I work hard on it. A man who looks like a professor comes into my office and wants to talk with me. He says he is familiar with my work and has been impressed. He wants me to change jobs—to come and work for him.

There are many possible ways to proceed in the interpretation of this dream. For example, it could be prophetic; perhaps someone will soon offer the dreamer a new job. Or the dream may have come merely to reinforce the good work the dreamer had been doing. However, in this example the dreamer chose to work with it in terms of contrasting ideals. He identified two key symbols which he felt represented major motivating forces in his life. The special project represented an ideal of commitment to and persistence in his current job; this was a force motivating him to stick with his work even when it became uncomfortable. The visiting man represented, in the dreamer's opinion, an ideal of change, a desire to try something new. At this point it is important to note that the dream does not choose between the ideals. Rather, it merely depicts them clearly in images. In waking life the man may have been having vague feelings of restlessness with his work, and the dream serves to clarify the situation and describe his alternatives. In this case the dreamer decided that the ideal of commitment and persistence was currently best for him. He had previously chosen the words "loving service" to define his overall spiritual ideal, and the attitudes of commitment and persistence seem to correspond well to this spiritual ideal. Of course, the real interpretation of the dream was his application of this decision—his efforts to actually hold in mind these chosen ideals, even on days when things were not going well at the job.

The second manner of comparing ideals is illustrated in the following dream, which a father had. This time we will see that the choice presented is not between alternative ideals depicted in the dream; rather, it is a matter of comparing a *dream ideal* to the *best ideal* that he consciously knows.

> My 14-year-old son appears in my secretary's office. He is smoking a cigarette, which greatly upsets me, although initially I don't show it. I ask him to leave and follow him. Once outside the office I say sarcastically, "You know that cigarette makes you look like a real fool!" He throws the cigarette down and goes down the back staircase crying. I feel sorry for having handled things like that.

The dreamer identified the primary motivating forces of his actions in the dream to be outrage and criticism. Although the dream ends with an attitude of guilt and remorse, it concerns not so much the dreamer's attitude toward his son as it does how the dreamer feels about himself. Since he felt strongly that the dream was a message about his relationship to his son, a particular approach was required. It involved comparing the ideal he was expressing in the dream to the one he most wanted to manifest in that relationship. Fortunately, he had previously written out his ideals for this relationship, so making the comparison was a simple matter. He had written the words "supportive" and "kind" as mental ideals and "regularly initiating creative projects to do together" as a physical ideal. It was clear from the comparison that the motivating influence shown in the dream fell far short of the ones he had already chosen as best. This evaluation brought an immediate awareness of the need to change his recent critical attitudes toward his son.

A further step can also be completed with this interpretation method. It involves using the *imagination* in the waking state to "redream" the events up to the point at which the response was not in keeping with the best ideal. At that point in the redreaming experience, the dreamer substitutes a new, more constructive response on his part and allows his mind, in reverie fashion, to develop a new ending to the dream. The following is the imaginative experience that resulted when the father employed this technique.

> Once again I saw my son in my secretary's office. He was smoking, but now I chose to have a more understanding attitude. I called to him to come into my office and we began to talk. I didn't mention the cigarette, but soon he brought up the topic. He said that he really didn't like doing it, but the other kids were doing it and he felt obliged to go along. He wanted my ideas on whether I thought he should stop. I came out of the dream at that point. Getting my opinion across to him didn't seem to matter much to me any more. I felt very good toward him for having asked me what I thought.

Such redreaming is a powerful technique when done in the context of selecting more positive responses to the dream events. In itself it is not dream interpretation. However, it can help us to *rehearse* new response patterns whose application *is* the real interpretation.

A final interpretive technique involving ideals concerns setting ideals in regard to the characters and circumstances we dream about. This is an especially valuable technique because it can be applied to nearly every dream we have, no matter how bizarre or enigmatic. The procedure rests upon the assumption that a dream often comes for the purpose of making us more aware of something. Another way of saying this is that a dream is often trying to call our attention to something we have ignored or perhaps misunderstood. This is borne out by the fact that many dreamers who report recurrent dreams find that once they finally become aware of the message being transmitted, the dream stops happening.

This assumption about a dream's function is important to almost any interpretive approach. What is surprising about the Cayce dream readings, however, is the frequency with which the characters and circumstances depicted in the dream are interpreted as actually being related to those same people and conditions in daily life. In such cases, there is likely to be a hidden message or lesson in the symbols and action of the dream. Throughout this book we will be exploring approaches for extracting and applying that meaning. However, there is a second perspective of those dreams that literally concern the people and conditions they portray. It may well be that some of these dreams are merely trying to *call attention* to certain aspects of our lives. It may be that in some dreams the most significant message is "Look closely at the parts of your life depicted here! You're not seeing them properly, or not seeing them at all." Perhaps the call of many a dream is to examine more closely the *relationship we have in waking life* with the things we dream of.

There is no better way to begin that examination than to consider our ideals. Let us use a hypothetical dream to see how this might be done. Imagine a woman who dreams that she is at her job and her supervisor, Mrs. J., comes into the office. The dreamer is expected to produce a report that she has been working on for several weeks, but she does not seem able to find it for her supervisor. The dreamer becomes extremely upset and frustrated with her own inability to locate the report, and then she awakens.

Suppose that the dreamer works with this dream using a variety of techniques but finds none that produces a satisfactory explanation of the dream events. She is left with the possible interpretative approach that the dream may have come simply to point out a need to examine certain aspects of her life. At least three things seem to be candidates: her relationship to Mrs. J., her relationship to her job, and the way that she deals with frustrating circumstances (of any nature). A worksheet resembling a grid would be useful for the dreamer at this point. At the top she would write the word or phrase previously chosen as her spiritual ideal. In each of two columns she would write specific ideal mental attitudes and ideal physical actions in regard to these specific aspects of her life. Her completed worksheet might look like this:

Spiritual Ideal: Healing Love

Relationship or condition	Ideal mental attitudes	Ideal physical actions
Mrs. J.	thoughtfulness; respect; cooperation	pray for her daily; frequently smile and speak in a pleasant way
Job	appreciation; consistency	be there on time daily; help fellow employees with their work when possible
Frustrating circumstances	patience, sensitivity to the lesson to be learned	take a few moments to pray

Of course, with this or any interpretaion method, the subsequent application of what has been discovered or observed is critical. In this case, the dreamer would then make a special attempt to apply these particular mental and physical ideals during the next few days.

We can see that this is an extremely useful tool for working with our dreams. Since even the most experienced student of dreams occasionally has a dream experience that seems nearly impossible to interpret with more conventional methods, this approach can likely be used by everyone. We should probably not begin our work on a dream with this technique, but rather save it for last. Even though it is one which has immediate application in daily life, some dreams will have a far more complex message than *just* encouragement to re-examine our ideals.

Summary

When we consider how important ideals are to nearly every topic in the Cayce readings, it is not suprising that they play a central role in our approach to dream interpretation. Since the process of interpretation is often a matter of reversing the work that went into the creation of a dream, it is especially important to note that ideals play a role in the *formation* of dream experiences. Not only does the perfect Ideal within us provide an impetus to experience inner worlds, but the Ideal and our conscious ideals *interact* in the creation of a dream experience. The readings further suggest that our capacity to *recall* a dream is closely tied to our attunement with the Ideal.

A variety of methods are available to us for using our personal ideals in the interpretation of a dream. First, we can examine the symbology of a dream with the notion that each symbol is a representation of a motivating force or ideal which we relate to in some way. Occasionally, the highest Ideal itself may be depicted in our dreams. Second, we can measure our attitudes, emotions and active responses to the dream events against what we hold in mind as our ideals. Particularly through the exercise of redreaming—a type of reverie experience—we can rehearse the transformation of responses which do not measure up to our best ideals. And finally, we can use the images of a dream to stimulate us to examine more closely particular aspects (relationships and conditions) of daily life. This examination involves setting mental and physical ideals in regard to the people and circumstances we dream of.

Ideals will play a key role in the subsequent chapters of this book. They provide a foundation for every stage in the systematic approach to growth described in the readings. As we use that approach to develop further steps in dream interpretation, we will frequently employ the perspective our ideals provide.

Exercise in Application

Select a dream which includes several people you know from waking life, as well as actions or feelings in the dream that do not measure up to your personal ideals.

Construct a chart similar to the one presented in this chapter. That is, write a word or phrase at the top of a page which will represent your spiritual ideal. Then make three columns. In the first one, write the names of the dream characters. In the second and third columns write mental and physical ideals respectively.

For example, for the first dream character, consider your waking life relationship. Suppose that this particular dream has come primarily to call your attention to the relationship and the need to clarify your ideals. Write down ideal mental attitudes and ideal physical actions for your interaction with this person.

Complete this process for each dream character. Then select one of the characters and share with your group what you have written as ideals. Allow others in the group to share in the same way. Take a period of two to three minutes for silence and during that time have a reverie in which you see yourself living out those same mental and physical ideals. Finally make a commitment to yourself that during the coming week you will make special efforts to live those ideals in the relationship. At the end of a week share your experiences with the group.

Chapter Six
FELLOWSHIP: OUR SOCIAL LIFE AT NIGHT

There is a tendency among certain practitioners of modern psychology to label as naive or unsophisticated the suggestion that the characters in our dreams may represent themselves. Some psychologists and dream theorists would argue that the dream is totally a depiction of internal processes of the dreamer. For example, they might say that when one dreams of a friend named John it undoubtedly symbolizes a part of one's own nature that resembles John. According to this view, to imagine that John literally represents himself would be to psychologically project one's own makeup onto him. At best, John might symbolize the dreamer's own attitudes toward him or the dreamer's feeling about their relationship.

In contrast to this approach, the Edgar Cayce readings indicate that there is, in fact, a social dimension to dreaming. Not necessarily all of our dream characters should be interpreted literally, but some dreams are likely to give us direct information or experiences involving the minds of others. Such an exciting possibility opens opportunities for us—through our dreams—to explore a profound kind of love and sensitivity to others. In the growth sequence of the Cayce readings this is called *fellowship*.

We might ask ourselves what evidence there is to refute the notion that all dream characters are only parts of ourselves. On the one hand, there is a wealth of anecdotal evidence of dreamers who seem to have received literal messages from others through their dreams. In these cases, information about the life and circumstances of one person is apparently transmitted to the sleeping mind of another. Perhaps "transmitted" is not the best term, because there are those who feel that the recipient (i.e., the dreamer) in such communication is actually the active party—moving out mentally to initiate contact with others.

Although such anecdotal stories are rarely convincing to skeptics, they are quite evidential to the dreamer. This writer has had a number of personal dream experiences which seemed to suggest the possibility of communication with others through this means. For the most part they have concerned people with whom there was a close emotional bond or whom I was formally or informally involved in helping (e.g., counseling). One example concerns a fourteen-year-old boy whom I had known for several years through our involvement in a youth group. He seemed like a rather quiet and unmotivated boy, somewhat lacking in initiative or positive self-concept. These characteristics were mysterious to me and largely frustrated my attempts to be helpful to him. I had known his family for some time and saw no clear link between his personality and his home situation. I had placed his name on a personal list of individuals for whom I was praying each day, and one night I dreamed of him. In the dream he rode up to me on his bicycle and began to talk to me. Realizing that I was dreaming, I remarked to myself on the clarity of his image and was astounded at how "real" he seemed to be. Upon awakening I remembered clearly the content of what he said to me. It concerned why he had a rather withdrawn unmotivated personality. He described certain experiences and attitudes he had toward his father and how they had led to his current condition. Later I was able to check with his mother and she validated the content of this dream message. I had apparently had an experience of fellowship in my dream: a contact with a deep layer of another, which led me to greater sensitivity and helpfulness to that one person.

As dramatic as such instances can be for the dreamer, there is a second body of evidence for actual contact with others in dreams, and this evidence is more generally accepted. Careful research in dream telepathy supports the concept of "mind-to-mind communication" between persons during sleep. This work is well documented by Krippner, Ullman and Vaughan in an excellent book entitled *Dream Telepathy,* which recounts ten years of systematic, scientific study of this phenomenon. In a typical experiment carried out in the dream laboratory, the subject would sleep in a specially prepared room with apparatus attached to his body to allow constant measurement of certain bodily functions (e.g., brain waves). In another room, a sender would be given a randomly selected target picture—often a reproduction of an art masterpiece—and would be asked to concentrate his attention on the target, trying to "send" it to the subject, who would incorporate it into his dream. In many cases the subject would be awakened at what seemed to be an optimal time and would be asked to recite or record any dream which he could recall. Several methods of scoring can be employed in such experiments. One approach is to ask the receiver at a time soon after his dream to compare his account of it to several pictures (perhaps five), one of which had been the target picture. The subject then ranks the pictures in his order of preference regarding how well each of them seems to match his dream experience. If dream telepathy were not possible, we would expect that over a great number of experimental trials the lucky guesses would be balanced out by the incorrect ones. However, in most of the extensive studies done by the authors and their colleagues there was convincing statistical evidence for telepathy in dreams. Subjects were consistently able to match their dreams to the images being sent to them by other persons.

Principles of Dream Telepathy

The Cayce readings contain many interpretations which point to a social dimension to our dream lives. We will examine some examples of this later in this chapter. In addition to these specific interpretations, we also find the underlying principles related to literal dreaming of key persons from our waking lives. First is the overall posture that the Cayce readings take toward dream study. We are warned against becoming reclusive dream examiners—using dream study merely to give self-gratifying attention to our own personalities. Certainly this is a strong caution that we might expect, since the readings never recommend that we become involved in *any* course of action or discipline if it is only for ourselves. We do well to approach dreams, or anything else, with a willingness to use what we obtain for the betterment of all life. This message is clearly stated in the following passage, which, although it does not specifically mention direct contact with others in dreams, does indicate that dream study involves responsibilities in our social interaction.

Hence the warning: Make practical all such dreams in the material experiences with others. And know that if they do not produce creative influences and better associations in thy home, in thy relationships with thy fellow men, something is wrong with same!　　　　　　　　　　**2419-1**

With this first basic principle in mind—the capacity of dreams to better our associations with people—we can see why one reading relates writing down dreams to helping others. This passage might provide some people with a genuine motivation for recording dreams. If one cannot get excited about dream study for purposes of understanding *oneself* better, it may be more motivating to think in terms of a practical approach to *helping our friends and family.* For example, many a parent has found dream telepathy to be an effective communication tool that can enable them to express more sensitive and loving helpfulness to their children.

. . .and the entity should keep a record of its dreams. For these *are* a means, a manner of expression that may be applicable in the experiences of being helpful to others; enabling the entity to warn others as well as self. . . 2346-1

A second principle which underlies telepathy through dreams concerns the nature of the unconscious mind. The readings postulate that all subconscious minds are in contact with one another. This concept suggests that the capacity to communicate with others in dreams is not limited to a few especially gifted dreamers, but is an innate ability of all of us. It further implies that a quality of oneness is not limited to just the superconscious mind—the Infinite or Divine within us; at the subconscious level of memory and deep personality patterns there is also a type of oneness. It is here that we have access to inner avenues of sharing and responsibility for each other.

We are probably fortunate that there is a law governing that access; otherwise, dream telepathy might become only a matter of invading someone's privacy. Contact with the mind of another through dreams is to a large measure made possible by an attitude or ideal consistent with the spirit of oneness. In a word, this means *caring.* One reading calls it a "love intent"; but no matter what terminology is used, the law of mind is the same. If one's ideal is selfishness, the source of the dream experience is likely to be one's own subconscious images of another, and not a genuine inner contact through the dream. However, as one's ideal comes from sincere concern and care for others, the subconscious pathways of oneness can open. Occasionally the required love intent may come from deep within the soul rather than from the personality. We may dream of someone we rarely think of and discover that the dream contains a profound message about that person's life. In such experiences we receive a gift—an intimation of the oneness between our own souls and that of another—and we are encouraged to live out the spirit of love and care that our dream has revealed.

There is a final principle related to this kind of dream experience, and it has to do with the kind of communication we might expect. It almost goes without saying that dreams which are actually about the characters they depict serve to make us aware of something which we have not yet understood.

Sometimes it will be about our relationship to them; in other cases it will concern physical, mental or spiritual aspects of their makeup. Such information is a responsibility with which we are entrusted. Knowing another person more deeply through a dream will, it is to be hoped, provide an impetus for closer fellowship in waking life.

In addition to this perspective, telepathic dreams also provide us with information about ourselves. We should expect this type of communication to reveal how our own way of living affects those around us. For example, one reading (294-139) explains a vision Edgar Cayce himself had. In the interpretation is the suggestion that Cayce get rid of behaviors which, although they might not have been serious hindrances to him, were causing difficulties for those around him. This final principle suggests that we should have an open mind in trying to understand a dream of fellowship. In many cases that dream will simply reveal information we need to know about a particular person; but in other cases it may instruct us in the quality of our interaction with him or the way in which our life patterns influence him.

Interpretation Tools for Telepathic Dreams

There is probably no simple method to determine whether or not a dream character represents an aspect of the dreamer's own personality or the literal person depicted. However, Cayce *frequently* interpreted dream characters in a literal fashion, so it is probably wise for us at least to consider this possiblity for most dreams. It may well be that many dreams have multiple interpretations—the dream characters may represent both themselves and parts of ourselves.

Some dreamers have discovered personal ways of recognizing telepathic contact with another through dreams. They have determined certain qualities of a dream which give significant clues that this is happening. When these characteristics are evident they can feel sure that at least one interpretation of the dream directly concerns the person depicted. Examples of these qualities are particular vividness of the dream, little dream action except for a conversation, and a sense of urgency upon awakening. This is *not* to say that your own criteria for determining a telepathic dream will match these examples. Each dreamer must learn over a period of study and evaluation what dream qualities are personal clues. And even after discovering these key indicators, one should not assume that every dream of a telepathic nature will necessarily announce itself with these characteristics. A quite ordinary dream may occasionally contain information which can be used in daily life to help a person who appeared in that dream.

A series of questions provides us with a direct approach to the study and evaluation of our dreams for evidence of this type of inner fellowship. With each question we will examine some instances from the Cayce dream readings in which that particular question was applicable.

Are both the characters and content of this dream literal? In some telepathic dreams there is a direct experience with another soul such that the content or meaning of the experience is not clothed in symbology. The example cited earlier in this chapter, concerning the withdrawn fourteen-year-old boy, is probably an instance of this type of dream telepathy.

Cayce's interpretation of a pair of dreams concerning the dreamer's mother suggests this type of literal *content and character.* The following is an account of the first dream:

Q-6. Saw my mother [106] and felt some foreboding that some such catastrophe might occur to her. Voice: "She thought she could be happy with you, particularly since [your wife] started being nice to her, but now she feels it better to return to her mother." Her mother is dead.   900-294

The interpretation indicates that this is a dream of warning: the dreamer's mother may soon die. He is warned "Be careful that in these fainting or these unconscious spells that may occur soon—*soon*—to the entity, she is in a way in which they may be easily cared for, see? That is, do not allow her to be alone very often, see?" (900-294, A-6) Apparently his mother survived that crisis period, because shortly thereafter the same dreamer submitted another dream to Cayce. Again it was interpreted in terms of literal character and content. In this case the account read, "Dreamed I gave a check to my mother for $500, and dated it one day ahead, and some trouble came up about it." (900-298, Q-1) The reading stated that the dream concerned his relationship to his mother and that unless he was more careful about how he handled financial transactions with her, difficulties would arise in their relationship.

These two examples make it all seem simple. Certainly not all dreams are so quickly solved, but this is probably a good place to begin with any dream that includes a character from our daily lives. We simply ask ourselves, "Could this dream be showing me in a direct manner something about this person or our relationship?"

Are the characters of this dream literal, but the content symbolic? For most dreamers, the majority of dreams with a fellowship quality will probably fit this second category. If we continue in our case study of the previous dreamer and his mother, we find a good example. He reports that he was in the woods or a field with his mother and wife. They discovered a threatening snake and started running, panic-stricken. He observed his mother, who was running in a zigzag course and advised him to do the same. Following her direction, they all got away safely (900-81, Q-4). Although Cayce interprets the mother to represent herself, he does not suggest that the content of the dream is literal. That is, it is not a dream which says that the mother will be helpful in getting away from snakes. Rather, the content is symbolic. The snake represents those persons who would harm the dreamer in an "underhand manner," and the action of the dream shows that the mother's guidance or counsel would help him avoid potential harm. The symbolic content of a telepathic dream is sometimes revealed by answering the question, "In what light or in what role does this dream place the character depicted?" In this instance it places the mother in the role of a helpful counselor in the face of a threat.

To conclude our study of this mother-son relationship, let us look at the following dream, in which we see another instance of literal dream character but symbolic content.

Q-4. I was at some kind of affair, or in some home with my mother and the Eckhouses. A small fire broke out, to which I paid little attention, until it grew and assumed more dangerous proportions. Then I tried to stamp it out. The floor in that spot seemed to cave in. We all became frightened and sought to extinguish the blaze.   **900-253**

Cayce's interpretation indicates that fire in this case symbolizes rising temper or anger in his mother. We can see that the role which both the dreamer and his mother play is one of being threatened by a fire which is initially ignored. He is encouraged in Cayce's interpretation to be more aware of or sensitive to the anger which she may have inside herself.

In another case the same dreamer brought this experience to Cayce for a dream reading: "Dreamed of [my wife]—that she gave birth to one—to twins—to triplets—to one, two, three." (900-183, Q-2) Although the interpretation given indicates that the wife represents herself and their relationship, this dream was not prophetic of triplets to be born. Instead, the content is symbolic; the three children correspond to the physical, mental and spiritual dimensions of life which were being brought into balance through their relationship. The dream was the result of "the union of two minds made one in purpose," and the symbology of the number three could be seen as the sense of completeness that comes from two individuals uniting. This dream was no doubt very encouraging to both the dreamer and his wife!

Should I be seeing things in daily life from this dream character's perspective? As we progress through these first three questions, the content of the dream becomes less and less significant. In this case we ask ourselves to consider the possibility that a person in the dream represents himself but the essential point of the dream events is merely to call our attention to his point of view. The application of this third question is demonstrated in the dream of a 23-year-old woman. She reported dreaming of sitting around a table with others, eating chocolate cake. Then they all moved into another room, where she sat down on her mother's lap. She then observed another person, named Helen, who looked sad because she had no mother's lap to sit on (140-6, Q-1). Cayce's interpretation gave no indication that the specific content or symbols of the dream were important; instead it stated that the dream was a call to be more sensitive to Helen and others like her. The dream was pointing out a need to see things from Helen's perspective and to be more aware of what might be going on inside her.

Another example provides a unique interpretation of this type of literal dreaming of others. What is unusual about this instance is that the persons most significant to the dream's message are conspicuously *absent* from the dream events. However, it is just the fact that the dreamer noticed them as being missing that gives us the interpretative clue. In daily life he was missing the point of view of these people.

Q-1. . . .Saw my father-in-law and myself walking in the court of 270 Park Avenue. Seemed to emphasize the fact that my father-in-law and I were there without our wives. We seemed completely alone, and the actions of mother-in-law and my wife seemed to be equally felt. Some sound then woke me up.
A-1. . . .the entity should more perfectly view those conditions in the mind of the wife and mother-in-law, seeing them from their viewpoint, and gaining the knowledge from same of the actions regarding each, see?   137-28

Is this a dream I am having for someone else? Although this type of dream experience is rarely indicated in the Cayce readings, there are some very interesting examples in which the bond of fellowship between two individuals is so strong that one literally receives a dream message for the other. We might expect this to happen most frequently in situations in which there is a strong ideal of helping and serving each other and in which one person is somehow blocking an important message from his unconscious.

One man dreamed he was in school and a lady teacher said to his brother, who was also in the class, "I haven't seen your hand up lately." The interpretation given by Cayce (900-64, A-3) indicated that this was a dream message *for* the brother. Through the attunement of subconscious forces, the dreamer was able to have a dream not just about his brother, but, in a sense, for him. The meaning of the dream was that the brother was failing to gain knowledge as he should, and Cayce's comments ended with the word, "Heed." Perhaps still not sure if the dream was just telepathically *about* his brother or was actually *for* his brother, the dreamer asked a follow-up question concerning to whom the injunction "Heed" was given. The response from Cayce made it clear that this was in fact an unusual dream, one that was received *for* the brother: "'Heed,' was and is given as a warning to the brother." (900-64, A-4)

In one other example of this type of dream a woman received a message for her husband: in five weeks he would have an especially meaningful contact with his deceased father.

Q-5. Saw five chrysanthemums on the grave of [my husband's] father.
A-5. In five weeks, then, there will be presented to [your husband] that lesson from the father that will bring the greatest joys to the life.   **136-16**

These two examples raise the provocative question of whether or not we should tell our dreams to those who seem to appear in them. This question is especially pertinent to instances in which we suspect that we have received *for* another person. However, it is also a dilemma when we feel we have simply dreamed *about* someone. The problem concerns our purposes in doing this. We may be attempting a subtle kind of manipulation—even unconsciously. If we cannot get a friend to do what we think is best by telling him in waking life, will he be more convinced if we tell him we dreamed it about him? And if so, how do we deal with the possibility that the dream may merely reflect our own desires or wishes (a topic to be covered in a later chapter)? The closest that the readings come to answering this question of sharing our dream messages with others is found in the following passage.

Q-5. Are the messages that come for individuals when seeking for them, in my dreams and meditations, of the spirit of truth? and should they be given to these individuals?

A-5. As has been indicated, as ye hold fast to Him, knowing all power is of Him when not turned to self in any manner, to be sure these should be given—whenever they come; but force never the issue. Let the Spirit of the *Christ* guide thy hand. Let that thou hearest, thou sayest, come as *His* message to such seekers—through *thee* only as a channel of blessings! 540-3

In essence, this seems to say that generally we should go ahead and share the dream, but we should be willing to drop the subject immediately if the other person shows no signs of wanting to pursue the discussion. Of course, there may be cases in which it seems reasonably clear that the dream character only represents an aspect of ourselves. In such a situation it might be misleading to tell the dream as if we really believed it to be telepathic. In addition to the rule to "force never the issue," we should remember to "Let the Spirit of the Christ guide thy hand." When in doubt about telling a dream to a person who appeared in it, take time for prayer and meditation about the matter. Make a tentative decision for or against doing so—making sure that that tentative decision is in keeping with your ideal—and then in prayer and meditation ask for guidance on whether or not you have decided properly.

Am I being treated by persons in the dream the way I treat them in waking life? We might call this the "tables-are-turned" function of a dream. A dream in which we are being treated unfairly by a specific person may be giving us information about our relationship with that very individual. With this question we ask whether or not the dream is merely drawing our attention to the type of treatment we are giving that person in daily life. An especially clear example of this is found in the following passage.

Q-2. *Henry Echatzkin and I were in the smoking room of the Stock Exchange and he was making fun of me because of my beliefs. I replied to him roughly and told him some of his actions were far more disgusting than the peculiarity, seemingly, of my convictions. He became very sarcastic.*
A-2. . . . Then, in applying this condition to the self as a lesson, the entity should see and know (mentally) that, as this is obnoxious to self in criticism by others of entity's convictions and of entity's tenets, same may be as obnoxious to others for entity to criticize *their* beliefs. 900-234

In other words, the dream had a literal aspect concerning Henry Echatzkin and his relationship to the dreamer. The experience that the dream provided was a chance to see and feel what it was like to receive the kind of treatment he had been giving Henry and apparently many other people as well.

Summary

A special contribution of the Cayce dream readings is their recognition of the possibility that dreams can be a channel for interpersonal communcation. The fundamental character of this process is described in the readings: (1) dreams can allow us to better our associations with others, (2) the nature of mind is such that all subconscious minds are in contact with each other, and (3) a variety of possible types of dream communication—or telepathy—are available. The law governing this process states that valid contact with another soul through dreams is determined largely by purposefulness. As we foster a sense of service and love, we enhance the likelihood of dream fellowship.

We must be careful not to assume that we are experiencing dream telepathy every time we dream of a person. However, for almost every dream it is worth while to ask ourselves these questions, which will help us determine whether the dream should be interpreted literally:

> Are both the characters and content of this dream literal?
> Are the characters of this dream literal, but the content symbolic?
> Should I be seeing things in daily life from this dream character's perspective?
> Is this a dream I am having *for* someone else?
> Am I being treated by persons in the dream the way I treat them in waking life?

Of course, we still have the problem of deciding whether to answer yes or no to each of these five questions. The solution is this: answer Yes to a question if you can find a constructive way of applying the dream in your relationship to the person it depicts. A constructive method of application is one that is in keeping with your overall spiritual ideal and with your ideals for that particular interpersonal relationship. And do not forget that the dream may have more than one level of meaning. You may be able to answer Yes to several of the five questions *and* find another interpretation that treats the dream characters in a more symbolic way. This is especially important when we consider that not all of a given dream may be telepathic. Many dreamers have found instances in which the major portion of a dream concerns their own psychological makeup, but one small feature of the dream seems to involve telepathic contact with someone.

Finally, if we wish our dreams to fulfill their potential of helping us to better our associations with others, we must be willing to act upon the insights derived from these special dreams of fellowship. As we gain confidence in our own capacity to recognize this valuable dimension of dreaming, we will use it frequently to alter our thoughts and deeds in order to live more harmoniously with others.

Exercise in Application

Work with dreams you have recorded which include individuals you know from waking life. Find a dream that could potentially be interpreted as if the dream character literally represents himself or herself. Determine a constructive way of applying the dream in your waking life relationship and work on doing that. Also list qualities you see in that person. Be aware of how you are responding to those qualities—in that person and in yourself—as you apply the dream interpretation you have chosen.

Chapter Seven
PATIENCE AND THE DIMENSIONS OF DREAMING

People who have had profound inner experiences frequently characterize them as being ineffable. One is likely to hear such a person say, "The experience just cannot be put into words—it was a type of reality beyond our own." Perhaps what they are saying is that they had ventured into a higher dimension of reality, a level of experience with deeper texture and more variables than daily life. In the past decade a growing portion of our society has been introduced to these levels of mind, which seem to be beyond normal, rational thought. Some of the avenues to these levels are relatively safe, offering built-in self-regulation; one such approach is through meditation and prayer. Other pathways include varying degrees of threat to the sensitive balance of body, mind and soul; we might expect such dangers to accompany the use of hallucinogenic drugs. Whatever the path, however, the fact remains that our society is awakening to the realization that there is far more to reality than just this material plane of existence.

In order to understand what might be implied by higher dimensions of consciousness it is useful to explore the meaning of the word *dimension* itself. This term denotes a way of measurement. To say that something is two-dimensional simply means that in order to describe it accurately one must specify two measurements. For example, a bid in the card game of bridge is two-dimensional because one must specify both a number and a suit (e.g., four spades). A cubic block has three spatial dimensions. To describe it accurately we must indicate how much space it takes up in height, width and depth.

We shall see shortly what all of this has to do with dreams. But first we need to consider a concept from the readings: waking life in the material world is three-dimensional. Up until now our examples have been rather specific, limited things, such as a bid in bridge. We might wonder how something so extensive as daily life itself can be confined to dimensions. Nevertheless, if we go back to our definition—a way of measurement—we find that a dimensional description of life is not only possible but quite helpful.

In measuring our experiences in material life, the Cayce readings do not limit themselves to the traditional notion of height, width and depth; instead, they treat those three as submeasurements of one dimension, which is called space. Similarly, we can think of past, present and future as submeasurements of a single dimension called time. It should be clear to us that both time and space are fine candidates for inclusion among our three primary measurements of human experience. Anything that happens to us has qualities regarding *when* and *where* it occurs. But this leaves us with the problem of determining that third dimension. We might ask ourselves, "What is missing when I describe the things that happen in my life only in terms of when and where they take place?" The immediate answer is that the *why* of the experience is missing. Another way of saying this is that time and space do not necessarily give us a measurement of the purposefulness of the things that happen to us in daily life. It is the sense of *purpose* in life's events that keeps us from being simply mechanistic creatures.

It is extremely significant to note the word which is used in the readings to define this third dimension: *patience*. By it we mean far more than simply passive waiting. Instead, it signifies the whole quality of inner *response* to those life events which are presented in time and space. Of course, there is a vast array of possible inner responses available to us: frustration, joyfulness, anger, humility, and worry, to name just a few. It seems quite fitting that Cayce chose one of the highest possible types of inner response to label that entire dimension of experience.

Perhaps an example will be most helpful in clarifying how three-dimensional thinking allows us to analyze our lives. Imagine the following experience: A man is driving home from work, and notices on his car's clock that it is 5:40 P.M. Just two blocks ahead he sees another car inching forward into a somewhat blind intersection from a cross street. If that car were to continue forward it would move right into the path of our driver, who responds to this situation by honking his horn at the other car. Now, if we were to try to analyze this experience using Cayce's hypothesis of three primary dimensions, we would quickly be able to determine the time and space measurements; our driver honked his horn at 5:40 P.M. at the location of a particular intersection. A materialistic perspective of life would lead us to maintain that this is all we need to know. However, our theory from the readings suggests it is not enough. In order to understand fully the experience of a soul in materiality, we need to know what his inner response was to the event. Did he honk with a sense of "Get out of my way, you foolish driver!" or with a sense of kindness and thoughtfulness for their mutual safety? As drivers, we have probably all had experiences of both types!

This hypothetical example points out why we have associated the quality of purposefulness to the dimension of patience. The purpose of our lives in time and space is to experience opportunities to find the optimal types of inner response. This is precisely what the Eastern notion of karma can mean. A karmic condition—or one created by our previous thoughts and deeds—is an opportunity in time and space to find an appropriate response in the dimension of patience. It is at this point that our dreams can play a role. They can help us *to explore alternatives in the dimension of patience,* and they are especially good at this because they take place at a fourth-dimensional level!

In the next section we will examine just what the fourth dimension may entail; but for the moment consider the idea that having fourth-dimensional capabilities makes exploring the third dimension easier. For example, imagine yourself lost in a flat wilderness area, wandering around aimlessly. There is an optimal place for you to be—namely, at your campsite—but you cannot locate it. From one perspective this is like being in two spatial dimensions—the terrain is like a piece of paper or the surface of a table. However, suppose that you could add another dimension: imagine that you could go up. Perhaps by climbing a tower or using a helicopter you might move through a third spatial measurement, that of height, to get a new viewpoint. From a thousand feet up you might be able to spot your campsite; you could then come back down to the ground and walk to it. The principle here is that the exploration of an environment with a certain dimensionality is *enhanced* by adding a higher dimension. Applied to dreams, it says that our search to find the best inner responses to life (i.e., our exploration of the third dimension—patience) is enhanced by our experiences in the fourth-dimensional world of dreams.

Understanding the Fourth Dimension

Various schools of metaphysical thought have offered a variety of solutions to the problem of the fourth dimension. However, it is especially interesting to note the similarity of answers between the Edgar Cayce readings and the writings of the great Swiss psychiatrist, Carl Jung. The readings state that the "Best definition that ever may be given of fourth dimension is an idea." (364-10) Jung's phrase for the fourth dimension was "thought itself." Clearly these two sources are saying the same thing. A thought has qualities of form or image. When we think something, actual creation has taken place using the one, spiritual life force. In the words of the readings, "Mind is the builder" (or, as one mistaken translator of the readings once put it, "Mind is the carpenter").

If thoughts are things, we might ask, then why don't we see them? The answer is that their existence is not of the three-dimensional world. However, we do experience their reality quite directly. Our three-dimensional, material existence is essentially a projection or representation of the fourth-dimensional world of thought. The conditions of the physical world can generally be understood as an expression of our previous thought patterns. How we are thinking and feeling today is building, at a fourth-dimensional level, the reality that we will experience in the future. It is not surprising that dreams can give us a glimpse of likely future events, for *the content of our dreams is largely our own thought-form creations.*

Using the Dimension of Patience to Interpret Dreams

From the previous abstract discussion let us turn now to some more practical techniques of working with our dreams. These concepts—although complex and difficult to understand fully—do provide us with an important key for unlocking some dreams. Recall our basic hypothesis from the examination of dimensions: Dreams, with their capacity to probe the fourth-dimensional world of ideas, can help us to explore alternatives in the dimension of patience.

Daily life constantly presents us with opportunities in time and space to find the best possible type of inner response. We are often tested at the points where we are weakest, at the points where we have the greatest tendency to react in an unloving or selfish way. Because dreams can move through the vast storehouse of all our thought memories (i.e., they are able to move through the fourth dimension), they can often discover for us the optimal attitude or feeling when that inner response has eluded our conscious search. In other words, dreams can serve to help us master the dimension of patience. We can ask ourselves a pair of questions about a particular dream to see if it is serving such a function.

Does the dream create an experience to awaken in me a quality of response needed in daily life? As improbable as it may seem to a seasoned symbol interpreter, this can happen in some dreams. The complex events and symbols of the dream may not be worth unraveling if the purpose of the experience was simply to stimulate a new feeling or response to life. Of course it is a tricky business to determine if this was in fact the purpose of a particular dream. The key phrase in helping us decide is probably "quality of response *needed* in daily life." Once we identify the kind of response the dream events awakened, we can ask ourselves whether or not it seems to answer a need in our daily life. If not, then it will be best for us to try another approach in working with that particular dream. If the answer to this question is Yes, then the real interpretation comes as we find ways of living that newly awakened attitude or feeling in our conscious experiences.

To see how a dream can move fourth-dimensionally to help a person master the dimension of patience, consider this hypothetical example. Imagine a college student who is having a difficult time in his freshman year. He is not used to being away from home and the requirements of his studies occasionally seem overwhelming. As we might expect, he is having trouble with the dimension of patience; his response to life events in time and space is one of frustration and doubt. Then one night he has a dream. In the sleep state his awareness is capable of moving through the storehouse of ideas, thoughts and memories. It can potentially draw upon any response quality that he has ever experienced in life. In his dream the student discovers it is graduation day. He is to receive his diploma in front of his friends and family. With a great sense of accomplishment he receives this award in the dream.

The student awakens with a great sense of well-being, although sorry to find it was only a dream. And yet, whereas he had gone to sleep with feelings of doubt and frustration, now he feels a new sense of confidence and hope. The dream has stimulated a better response quality to the opportunities he faces. Somewhere among the fourth-dimensional patterns within his soul there was one of hope. With his conscious mind he had not been able to find it; but the dream state provided an experience to help reawaken a feeling of hope in him.

Another good example of this process is found in the readings. The dream of one woman [136] was quite simple: "[My husband] was in grave danger of some kind and I saved or rescued him." (900-216, Q-18) Cayce's interpretation does not indicate that this is precognitive of imminent danger to the husband, nor does it attempt to translate the symbol of her husband or the events. It says instead that the dream is demonstrating to her the attitude that she should be holding in mind toward her marriage: "that attitude to meet the needs of the other." In other words, we can see this as a dream concerned with the dimension of patience. The events of the dream

100

stimulate a particular response quality within the dreamer's mind.

A further example of this nature concerns the following dream:

Q-9. My mother was in a faint—unconscious. She and I were in the same house. I was very frightened and tried to get a doctor. Finally some doctor's assistant came, and as he and I went into Ma's room, I found she opened her eyes and took my hand, but was very sick.   900-216

If we were to ask what response is awakened by these dream events, our initial answer might be "fright." However, it is unlikely that the dreamer would have seen this as a *needed* reaction in his daily life. When we look at the dream more closely, we find a second answer: the desire "to get help." This points out that in using this technique we must explore all the responses which are awakened, for in some cases the dreamer's most obvious response to what the dream attempts to offer may be inappropriate (as in the bumble bee dream cited earlier). In the above example the reading suggests that it is the second reaction, that of seeking help, which was the point of the dream. This individual needed to be responding to his life circumstances with more of a willingness to try to get help from within. The interpretative passage reads: "Then, as there is sought the physician for the sick . . . then the entity should seek, through those forces from within self, that there may come the understanding . . . " (900-216, A-9)

Does the dream allow me to rehearse a response quality which I already know is best? Frequently we know we need improvements in the dimension of patience, and we know just what the optimal response would be. However, it may be only an intellectual knowing. If we have not found the willpower actually to apply the alternative response, we still need help. This is where a dream comes in. A dream can create events which give us the opportunity to experience how it feels to respond in a way that we have suspected would be best.

This principle is well illustrated in the example of a man who had been working with meditation and dream study for ten years. He had observed one particularly troublesome life condition—a frequent response pattern within himself which was not in keeping with his ideals. He found that whenever he met an attractive woman he fantasized a sexual involvement with her, although it was not his manner to act on these inward responses. For him this was a struggle with the dimension of patience. After a time he received a dream that helped him in this conflict.

Even before the dream, this man had decided that the best response toward an attractive woman was one of caring, yet not imagining physical involvement. Despite the fact that he had intellectually decided on the response he wanted to experience, he found it very difficult to react in this way. The old, deeply ingrained pattern was hard to overcome. Then he had an opportunity to rehearse in the fourth-dimensional world of dreams the very response to women which he had hoped to experience.

> I am on a trip with many other people. There is a sense of adventure. We seem to be on some large type of public transportation. I have the feeling that we will soon be at our destination and our group will be staying together in a hotel. A beautiful young woman in our group comes over to me and suggests that we plan to sleep together at the hotel. I know immediately that I will say no, but want her to understand that I am not rejecting her as a person. I carefully decline, in a way that I hope keeps her from feeling that something is wrong with her.

There are many possible ways to approach this dream. One especially interesting feature is that the thought-form image of the woman has adopted the aggressive characteristic that the dreamer had given it in his previous fantasies. Rather than directly explore this factor or the other symbols, he felt strongly that it was the very response quality itself in the dream that was the interpretation. His ability actually to respond to a beautiful woman in this way had made a deep emotional impression on him. The rehearsal quality of the dream served as a breakthrough and a reminder that he could master the dimension of patience in his dealing with women in waking life.

Summary

Cayce's theory of the dimensions of human experience is helpful to our understanding not only of material life but of our dreams as well. The three primary dimensions or measurements of time, space and patience are complemented by a fourth dimension of ideas or thought itself. From one perspective, we can say that our work in the earth as souls is to master the third dimension: the quality of our responses to life situations. In learning to manifest the most loving types of response, we also master the dimensions of time and space.

Since dreams can be viewed as fourth-dimensional experiences—journeys into the world of thought forms—we find that they can be extremely valuable in our attempt to achieve mastery of the third dimension. There are at least two ways in which they can help us reach this goal: a dream can awaken a particular response pattern *needed* in waking life, or it can permit us a *rehearsal* experience with a response we already know is best. Our efforts to arrive at a helpful interpretation will be furthered if we question ourselves about a dream, checking to see if either of these two functions is being fulfilled. Although not every dream will fit this category, many a dream is an adventure in mastering the dimensions of inner life.

Exercise in Application

Work with a series of dreams, perhaps a week's worth; for each dream record the responses you made in the dream—attitudinal and emotional. For example, in one dream you might have been indifferent in one part of the dream, fearful in another part and appreciative in the final part.

Then go back and examine your lists of these responses, circling those which you feel ought to be experienced more often in waking life. Do any of them appear more than once? Select one for which you particularly feel a need in daily living. Discuss with a group the types of things you might be *doing* in life to increase the likelihood of that particular response.

For example, suppose you chose the response of appreciation. In waking life you might find that in being more helpful to others you also become more aware and appreciative of what others do for you. Or, by making an effort to say "thank you" even when it is easier to say nothing, a genuine sense of appreciation may begin to emerge.

Whatever actions you decide on, with the help of your group, take a week and try applying them. Report back to the group on your results.

Chapter Eight
IN HIS PRESENCE: DREAMS OF DIVINE INSPIRATION

We have been promised that we can know God. The knowledge referred to is not just an intellectual understanding of His laws, but a direct, experiential knowledge of His love and presence in our lives. It is the experience that confirms our faith and rekindles a profound sense of purposefulness in our lives.

There are many avenues for this type of experience. For some it comes in prayer or meditation. For others, through an attunement to nature. However, for many it is primarily through the dream state that old perspectives of life are shed and a direct perception of the Divine is revealed. Such a dream can inspire us, in the deepest sense of the word. For days or weeks afterwards we are likely to see ourselves, others and daily life in a different way. We may be inspired to complete some new project. But in every case, life itself seems more holy, permeated with a sense of meaning and purpose. Discovering or rediscovering the promise of God's closeness is a primary benefit of dream study.

A Proper Approach

Occasionally we may have a dream of divine inspiration without conscious preparation on our part. However, it is much more likely for such a special dream experience to follow a period of personal attunement. That attunement may have many facets: improving physical health, meditating consistently and developing appropriate attitudes and ideals. It is this last feature that particularly requires clarification.

The Bible, the Cayce readings and many other sources suggest that God can be known by those who diligently seek Him. And yet it is the attitude or purpose accompanying that seeking which is critical. This principle was well illustrated for me in an experience with a large group of spiritual seekers. We had traveled to Egypt, and as a part of our activities we were to have a rare opportunity: to spend the night in the King's

Chamber of the Great Pyramid. All members of the group were familiar with the ancient metaphysical teaching that the Great Pyramid had been built thousands of years ago as a hall of initiation. In other words, the history as well as the very structure of the Pyramid was likely to induce a special kind of dream.

There was a tremendous sense of anticipation in the group as the day drew nearer for our chance to sleep in the Pyramid. Although there were many other activities in our month-long tour throughout the Middle East, many people—perhaps even a majority—felt that this was to be the highlight of the trip. There was a general feeling that some or all of us might have a breakthrough dream—an initiation into higher realms of consciousness.

However, as I talked with others and examined closely my own attitudes, I had the sense that something was not quite right. I realized that no matter how profound our desire might be for such a dream, this desire by itself was not enough. What was required was a proper attitude. It would not do merely to want something for ourselves. Rather, there had to be an attitude of *giving* of ourselves in devotion to our ideal. My strong feeling was that our group faced a paradoxical situation. Our strong desire to have a dream of His presence could stand in the way of its fulfillment. As long as we had an attitude of coming to this special place to *get* something for ourselves instead of *giving* of ourselves, it was unlikely that the experience would happen.

The importance of proper attitude and purpose was further clarified for me on the actual night we slept in the Pyramid. As I meditated before falling asleep that night in the King's Chamber, I felt a questioning within me: Would I be able to handle or integrate a profound dream experience if one were given to me tonight? In meditation I sensed an answer, or rather a principle that helped me answer my own question. The inner guidance indicated that a dream of divine inspiration could be given only if I had the personal psychological strength to keep quiet about it afterwards. I realized that it would be my tendency to want to tell others immediately if something happened to me that night. Perhaps that tendency came from some kind of anxiety that I imagined such a special dream might produce. But whatever the reason, I knew that first I had to resolve that I would attempt to keep any sort of deep experience to myself. A dream of His presence would not be given if I were merely going to dissipate the energy and inspiration by immediately talking about it. Perhaps months or years later it would be appropriate to carefully share it with others, but only after I had allowed it to do its work within me.

Interestingly, we find this very principle in the Cayce dream readings. Speaking of attunement and direct experience of the highest forces of the universe, he said, "Yes, these should be sought but rarely spoken of." (900-69) However, agreeing within oneself not to speak too soon of any dream of His presence does not ensure that the divine contact will be attained immediately. As a conclusion to my Pyramid story, I can report that even though I resolved to keep silent about any experience, I recalled no dreams from that night.

A final point should be considered in our understanding of the proper attitude for receiving a dream of divine inspiration. Perhaps it is so simple that it is taken for granted. We must believe that God's direct communion with us is possible. We must have a concept of God's nature as both transcendent *and* imminent. He is always ready to reveal Himself to us; and through our attitudes and "the manner of life [we] live . . . " (1968-10) the direct experience is made possible. This promise is clearly stated in the following reading.

Q-5. What is meant in my life reading by the statement that I would have imposing dreams and how can I best interpret them to be helpful to me in the present?
A-5. These have come, these may come. Ye interpret them in thyself, not by what others say, but dreams are presented in symbols, in signs . . . For the Lord's are oft spoken in dreams, in visions. For He is the same yesterday, today and forever. Be not unmindful that there is the manner of life ye live so that ye merit this or that experience.   1968-10

Dreams of Contacting God

The very title of this section may stimulate skepticism in some readers. Many of us are predisposed to doubt those who say they have just seen or spoken with God. Perhaps our cultural bias against accepting such reports has a historical origin. Looking back over the centuries, we find examples of destruction and pain brought on by one person or a few who said that God had spoken to them. Too many wars have been fought because of divine commandments of dubious validity. History is also full of examples of some people trying to control others under the guise of a divine instruction.

In our sophisticated society it is easy to find other explanations for dreams or meditation experiences that seem to be divinely inspired. Elaborate theories of personality provide us with quick answers to explain away what may have seemed like a contact with God. A psychologist or psychiatrist is likely to claim that when God seems to appear in dreams the experience is merely the result of an internalization of the authority figures of our past. And, although this might actually be the case in some instances, it is remarkable how often the Cayce readings encourage us to adopt another perspective. This material time and again returns to the principle that God is knowable, and that what seem to be dream experiences of His presence are likely to be just that.

The following two examples illustrate how God may meet us in a dream. In the first case it is through a voice.

Q-4. I had lost most of my worldly possessions. I was occupied in a capacity humble and looked down upon by many. I was disregarded. I was sweeping the dirty, wet sidewalks, trying to get them clean. This subconscious me viewed this physical me with pity. Finishing my task I took a Sunday newspaper and started for ... to see my mother. My recreation lay in that Sunday funny page—it was a frivolous moment or physical relief for the physically struggling mind. Fast I held to my ideals, trying not to complain and to manifest the highest and best within me, and to show others, if only they would listen. Then the voice spoke—and the Lord spake unto me and said: "But come, I will make you a promise. Such a promise have few men in the ages heard. Whilst thou are in the flesh, thou shalt labor and serve all man, but whenst thou art come into the Spirit, thou shalt be risen unto Me, yea even as the Christ, and thou shalt rule all of Man." 900-226

Cayce's interpretation and comments on this dream are lengthy and provide an elaboration of the final part of the dream. Little time is spent in his commentary on the question of how valid the experience was. There is a basic assumption that hearing the voice in the dream was a direct experience of God's presence. This raises the question of whether or not every dream voice that seems to be God's really is. A helpful procedure in making this judgment is to measure what the voice says against our highest ideal. God's voice will always call us to do the best that we know to do.

The second case is quite different from the first. In this example the dreamer actually meets a person whom he believes to be God. Remarkably, God turns out to be a businessman. Is it blasphemous for Cayce to have suggested that the experience with a businessman was a type of direct contact with God? Not if we see that this symbol is meant to represent only a partial picture of God's nature. Cayce's interpretation was not intended to degrade God, but instead to point out the potentiality of being human; its message was that the Divine can be expressed in all its fullness in an individual. Although the dream is quite lengthy, the reader is encouraged to look at it carefully. It is one of the most delightful dreams ever brought to Edgar Cayce, and it is also quite instructive in the encouragement it gives us to broaden our concept of what a dream of His presence might entail.

Q-1. Then our maid came in and said: "You should be close to the front door, for God may come in. He will enter that way." [137] and Ma paid little attention to her, but I perked up at once and started forward and then the maid announced the distinguished visitor—that "God" was calling upon us. I rushed out into the hall and towards the door. Halfway to the door I met God, and jumped for Him, throwing my arms around His neck and hugging Him. He embraced me. After that I noticed God's appearance. He was a tall, well-built man, clean cut and clean shaven, wearing a brown suit and carrying a gray derby hat. He had an intelligent look, an eye that was kindly but piercing. He had an expression that was firm and features clean cut. He was very healthy, robust, businesslike, and thorough, yet kindly, just and sincere. Nothing slouching, shuffling, maudlin, sentimental about Him—a man we might say we'd like to do business with. He was God in the flesh of today—a business or industrial man, not a clergyman, not dressed in black, not a weakling, a strong healthy intelligent Man, whom I recognized as the Man of today and whom I welcomed and was glad to see and I recognized in this fine upright Man—not the ordinary—but God. Then we passed my liquor closet—it was half open. God looked in—I showed Him the half-opened closet. But, I thought, I forget He is not the ordinary Man he looks but God and knows all, so I might as well show Him all, as pretend anything. So I opened the closet wide for Him to see. I showed Him my liquor, particularly the "Gin" which I used for cocktails. "In case of sickness," I said to God. "You are well prepared," God replied sarcastically. We proceeded into the parlor where the radio was still playing and [137] and Ma amusing themselves with it. I wanted [137] and Ma to meet God, but they couldn't seem to recognize Him. "Of course they would not know Him," I thought. "How could they recognize Him, when they have not the faith that He did appear in the flesh long ago in Christ . . . So they did not see, or at least pay any attention to Him. I sat down on the sofa to converse with Him. "You could work harder," He said. I almost started to reply, yet bethought me that God knew all—no use. I meekly assented. "You could hardly do less," He continued . . .   900-231

Dreams of a Spiritual Master

A dream of divine inspiration may depict a contact with a highly evolved soul or a being of light. As we might expect, the dreams of this category brought to Edgar Cayce usually involved the appearance of the Christ. In every case the reading was supportive of the validity of the experience—sometimes suggesting that the attunement may not have been perfect but that this was a dream of His presence.

In one example (137-127), a man relates that in his dream he has a general sense of the Master's presence. The events of the dream involve a pistol being fired at him, and he imagines himself being successful in stopping the bullet in its flight towards him. Cayce's interpretation indicates that this experience contains a valuable lesson concerning his relationship to the Master. The dreamer is told that as he realizes the ideals he has already set in regard to knowing the Master, the forces of nature (as depicted by the bullet) will become subservient to the forces of his inner self. Perhaps even more important, he goes on to ask this question:

Q-14. How can I call this presence?
A-14. Making thy will one *with* the Father, and in the silence—just the moment—just the seeking—just the *giving* of self *wholly* into the use of that desire to *know* the guidance of that will.   137-127

This answer informs us of several key factors in awakening a dream of the Master's presence: aligning our will with God's, learning to hold the silence (in meditation), learning to keep our awareness in just the present moment, having a strong sense of seeking, surrendering ourselves, and desiring to know His guidance.

In another and more direct contact with the Christ in a dream (900-315), the dreamer relates seeing a light which he knows to be another consciousness. It speaks to him, identifying itself as the Christ. Then the Master appears to him in white flowing robes and initiates a merging of consciousness into one. The dreamer experiences in that moment a deeper understanding of the Master's words. The next scene is one of trying to apply what he has just experienced. The Master takes him to a Palm Beach hotel where many wealthy, influential people have congregated. His dream report goes on to say:

We were in a Palm Beach hotel, full of wealthy influential people. I walked down the path with some who spoke and joked of women and I joined them. The Master passed before me and out of the gate. I should have followed Him, I know, but instead remained with these people, to whom I said: "I don't know anyone here, but I used to. I used to chase around with Robert Lehman," thus trying to make an impression on my friends about my previous influential companion . . .900-315

From this point the dream continues and becomes rather jumbled and troublesome. Contact with the Master is not reestablished.

Cayce's interpretation of this dream affirms the validity of the contact but points out an important lesson. The dreamer lost the companionship of the Master through the choice he made. He chose to be attracted to the "vicissitudes of the *worldly* conditions, even in the higher social position" and thereby lost the attunement he had had in the initial part of the dream.

This example makes it clear that in these special dreams of contacting the Divine Presence it is especially important to *respond properly*. There must be openness and trust (well-illustrated in the first portion of the preceding dream), but also a sustained kind of attunement. Even in such profound dreams we are likely to face choices which can either deepen our conscious oneness with the Christ or cause us to lose the attunement.

It is also important to consider the element of proper response *after* the dream is recalled. We have already seen the advisability of keeping quiet about these experiences, allowing them to be integrated into our waking life. Another appropriate response is *hope* rather than fear or anxiety. The question of proper response to a dream after it has occurred is brought out in the following passage.

Q-7. [413]: *Please give me the significance of the dream I had the night of Sept. 26th at which time I saw the Master.*

A-7. As there has been in self that seeking more and more for the material confirmation of the thought, the intent and the purpose of self's activities, so in that given, that seen, is a confirmation of that purpose, that thought, that activity.

Hence, rather than bring fears on the part of self, or anxiety as respecting those visioned in same, rather know that self is being led by Him who *is* the Guide, the Giver, the Promise to all mankind.   262-55

We have another example of a dream in which the dreamer reports seeing Jesus (900-114). The dreamer shouts to all about him "We can be like He—I have proved it!" However, no one will believe him. The dreamer then enters a grocery store and once again sees a man whom he feels is the Christ. A woman nearby says to the dreamer, "Isn't He a wonderful God?" Still intent upon his previous exclamation, he tells the woman, "You can be like He." But not especially convinced of this, the woman counters with, "Oh, you are not like He. You are a soft, mushy human." The dream concludes with painful questioning by the dreamer of why people will not believe his message. A voice at the end of the dream, seemingly from the Christ, reaffirms the rightness of his beliefs. Commenting on this dream, the Cayce reading says:

This, as we see, approaching that condition wherein the elements of the spiritual entity enter that almost of the Holy of Holies, gaining strength and wisdom from Him . . .
. . . this entity must give a message, that those who would seek Him, the Master, may find Him. 900-114

Finally, let us look at one of the most inspiring dreams of the Christ reported in the Cayce material, a dream that Edgar Cayce himself had. No reading was ever taken on it, but perhaps it was not necessary to do so; the experience seems to speak for itself. It is not the point of this dream to claim any special status for the man Edgar Cayce. In fact, we *all* have a special work to do in the earth, and any of us could conceivably have a similar dream. The message of this special experience of His presence seems to be that God is working with us—there is a plan for the earth and its people.

[12/12/42 P.M. or Sunday A.M. 12/13/42—Edgar Cayce dreamed:] I was sitting alone in the front room playing solitaire when there was a knock at the front door. It was dark outside but rather early in the evening. When I went to the door a gentleman whom I did not recognize asked, "Cayce, I want you to go with me to a meeting this evening." At first I said, "But I seldom go out of evening and my wife is here and it would leave her alone." But he insisted I should go with him and I did. As I went out I realized that another person was waiting for us in the street. We walked toward the ocean, but when we came to the ocean we walked on as if into the air, up and up, until we came to where there seemed to be a large circus tent. He said, "We will go in here." We approached the flap of the tent and as he pulled the flap back I, for the first time, realized that the two men with whom I had been walking were the evangelists Dwight L. Moody and Sam Jones. We entered a large, circular tent; a very ususual kind of light pervaded the place, something like an opalescent light. Many figures were there. All seemed to be shrouded, all dressed alike. Very few I remembered ever having seen before. Then to one side of the place—as more and more figures appeared, until it was full—it seemed that there was a large screen on that side, and as if there was lightning in the distance. With the lightning there was a noise, not of thunder but of wind, yet nothing seemed to stir; and there was no form with the brilliant flashes but as if a cloud, very beautiful. When I asked one of my companions what it was, I was told "The Lord our God will speak to us."

Then a voice clear and strong came as from out of the cloud and the lightning, saying, *"Who will warn my children?"* Then all was silent. Then again the same, *"Who will warn my children?"* Then, from out of the throng before the throne came the *Master,* but as if in the same garb of those about Him. He spoke saying, "I will warn my brethren." The answer came back, "No, the time is not yet fulfilled for you to return, but who shall warn my children?" Then Mr. Moody spoke and said, "Why not send Cayce, he is there now."

Then the Master said, "Father, Cayce will warn my brethren."

"And we will all help," came a grand chorus.

From *Dreams and Dreaming,* Part I, pps. 439-40 (Vol. 4 of the Edgar Cayce Readings Library Series)

The Unrecognized Christ in Our Dreams

Cayce once gave a rather remarkable answer to a question posed in a dream reading. It opens up an entirely different vantage point on knowing His presence in our dreams. Unfortunately, we do not have an account of the actual dream. Instead of submitting one, the dreamer simply gave the date of the experience and asked if it had been interpreted correctly. After an initial comment by Cayce, the dreamer asked, "Who was the strange man [in the dream]?" The reply was, "The Christ!" (307-15, A-3)

Could it be that unrecognized figures in our dreams may be the Christ? Perhaps because our attention is focused elsewhere in the dream, we frequently fail to notice His presence in our midst. The adage that we "oft entertain angels unaware" may apply not only to daily life, but to our dreams as well.

Related to this possibility of the unrecognized Christ is that of the unrecalled Christ in our dreams. Although there may not be examples of this recorded in the readings, my personal dream study convinces me of this possibility. Simply stated, it may be that we often encounter the Christ in a dream but fail to recall it in the morning. Although not conclusive, one piece of evidence for this is the occurrence of a healing during sleep. Many people have had the experience of being in a state of some dis-ease at the end of a day and praying before going to sleep for a healing by the Christ. Upon awakening, the person may discover that a release of the condition has occurred, and although nothing specific is remembered, there is a feeling of having been with Him.

In a similar fashion, a personal dream experience further convinced me of this possibility. I gradually awoke one morning and, while still in a hypnagogic state (the condition intermeditate between sleep and complete wakefulness), began to recall what seemed to be a very important dream. I realized at the same time that if I fully awakened too quickly, I would probably lose the recall. I picked what seemed to me to be the two key elements of the dream and focused my mind on them as I gradually became totally conscious. I found myself lying in bed repeating to myself, "In my dream I was with Mother and the Christ." Now fully awake and having brought back the symbol of my mother, I was able to remember in great detail what felt like the entire dream. Yet, in my conscious recall, nowhere did I remember the Christ's appearance! Although alternative explanations are possible, it is my belief that the dream had in fact included the Christ, but, due to some psychological block or filtering mechanism, His presence was not remembered.

Of course, an insightful variation of my conclusion is that the Christ was in the dream, but not in the image of a human form. Perhaps there is something in the *quality of interaction* in the dream events that indicates the presence of the Christ. Such a theory has been put forth by one student of the Cayce readings, G. Scott Sparrow (author of *Lucid Dreaming*). He points out that the intervention of the Christ in our dreams is not necessarily associated with the appearance of the man Jesus, nor even with some specific dream image such as a light. Instead, the Christ may influence our dreams by affecting the *process* of what is going on—as in, for example, an unexpected reconciliation or the overcoming of fear or animosity.

This probably represents the most important tool for working with our dreams described in this chapter. It gives us a way of looking at more ordinary dreams in terms of a contact with His presence. Certainly, the rare dreams of meeting God or the Christ face to face are dramatic and often transformative. However, God reveals Himself to us in the ordinary as well. We can identify His presence in our dreams by asking, "Do the events of this dream seem to be influenced by a movement toward greater wholeness and integration?" When we can recognize this influence, we discover that the Divine reveals itself frequently to us in the dream state. The following dream provides an example of how this approach to dream interpretation can work. We might understand this dream to show an influence of His presence. The reconciling and integrating movements in the dream are clear, even though the human form of the Christ may not appear.

> I'm in a dark, poor section of a city. A young man starts chasing me down an alley. I'm running for what seems to be a long time in the dream. Then I become aware that I am dreaming and that much of my dream life is spent running from male pursuers. I say to myself, "I'm tired of this never-ending chase." I stop running, turn around and walk up to the man. I touch him and say, "Is there anything I can do to help you?" He becomes very gentle and open to me and replies, "Yes. My friend and I need help." I go to the apartment they share and talk with them both about their problem, feeling compassionate love for them both.

Summary

Dreams can be a way of discovering the reality of God's promise that we can know Him directly. This type of dream is likely to require preparation on our part. In addition to consistent efforts at attunement, a proper attitude is needed. We should have not only an opening to such experiences and trust in their validity, but also a sense of giving of ourselves rather than getting something. It may well be that a willingness to keep silent about the experience is also a significant factor for some dreamers.

A dream in which we directly contact His presence may come in a variety of forms: a voice that seems to come from God, some symbolic representation of God (such as a light or some human form), or the image of a spiritual master (such as the Christ). Both during and after the dream, it is the quality of our response that is crucial. To realize the potential of such a dream we must maintain the attunement to and companionship of His presence, despite distractions in the dream that might lead us elsewhere. In the days following such a dream, our response should be one of hope and a willingness to share the *spirit* of the experience through our love for those around us.

His presence may also be felt in one's dreams even though it is not recognized immediately nor remembered. An especially important insight is that an influence of harmony and reconciliation in a dream can be viewed as the intervention of the Christ Spirit in one's consciousness.

Finally, it is well to keep in mind that we should not judge our own spiritual growth by how often God or the Christ seems to be appearing in our dreams. We would do well to remember the story of the apostle Thomas, whose doubting nature required that he see the physical image of Jesus directly. As he was told by the Master, "Now you believe because you have seen me? Blessed are those who have not seen me and have believed."

Exercise in Application

Make a personal list of qualities which you attribute to the Christ. Specifically include the types of *influence* which you can imagine the Christ having on your life. For example, you might list the influence of reconciliation with others and the influence of persistence toward an ideal.

If you are in a group, take a few moments at a meeting and have each member share the items on his or her list. Hearing the ideas of others may lead you to make changes in your own list. This exercise will probably work best if you have between six and ten types of influence in your personal list.

Then take a series of dreams—perhaps a week's worth—and look for instances of His presence, unseen yet active, in them. Underline portions of any dream that seem to be guided or influenced by one of the qualities on your list.

If there is time, allow each person in the group to share briefly an example in which he found evidence of His presence active in a dream.

Chapter Nine
ONENESS OF ALL FORCE: THE PSYCHIC ELEMENT OF DREAMING

After an interval of eight years, a woman dreamed of a man she had known in her school years. What seemed especially remarkable to her was the fact that she had never before dreamed of him—even in the period when she saw him frequently. She was especially skilled at dream recall, remembering one or more dreams every night. However, this dream seemed to have an unusual quality to it and she related it to several of her friends at work the next morning. In the dream she found herself in an airport. In the crowded terminal she suddenly saw the male friend from many years ago. She called to him and he turned around, acknowledging her presence, but then hurrying off, as if he had no time for her. Two days after this dream she received a letter from this man, written the same day the dream had occurred! It was their first communication in eight years and it had been preceded by this psychic dream. Although the friendship was subsequently renewed, it never developed into frequent contact because of the distance between their home towns and a hurried, busy lifestyle on both their parts.

The psychic element of dreaming is one of the most intriguing features present in the Cayce dream readings. Decades before the sophisticated research of parapsychologists had been reported, Cayce was pointing out the ways in which ESP often influences our dreams. In fact his readings sometimes identified the dream state as an especially good one to explore one's own psychic potential. The development of ESP through dreaming is mentioned in passages like this: "Dreams to this body are ... towards that development of psychic forces within self ... " (136-77) Recent parapsychological research has been supportive, not only of the dream as an avenue for ESP, but of altered states of consciousness as well. However, among all the varieties of expanded awareness available to us, it seems clear that none is more natural and readily accessible than the dream state.

ESP and the Principle of Oneness

Before examining approaches for identifying our own psychic dreams, some preliminary concepts are valuable. First we should consider the meaning of psychic ability itself. Is this a rare capability, possessed by only a few such as Edgar Cayce? And how does ESP work—through an undiscovered particle transmission, an unknown wave form, or some other channel?

The answers to these questions are found in the Cayce readings, and they have been summarized in a general theory of psychic ability, *Understand and Develop Your ESP,* by the present writer. In brief, this material suggests that ESP is a quality of the soul itself and therefore is at least a latent ability in everyone. Since we often draw nearer in attunement to the soul forces in dreams, for most people it is more likely that ESP will occur in the night than during working hours. However, we probably all use our psychic ability much more frequently than we realize. A hunch, intuition or feeling that influences a decision is likely to be ESP. Or, as recent laboratory research suggests, we may be using our psychic ability in waking periods in a rather unconscious way. It may be influencing our choices in daily life without our realizing it.

Concerning the mechanism of how it happens, Cayce's readings indicate that it is an inner process that involves the body, mind *and* soul—rather than a purely physical mechanism that would require merely a particle or wave to be the carrier of information. Of course, the question remains, "What is an 'inner process'?" The key to this theory is the reality of thought. We have already examined this basic concept: thought forms exist at the fourth-dimensional level (see Chapter 1). Apparently our awareness has accessible to it not only our own thought forms but those of others as well (i.e., telepathy).

However, this principle would not explain some of the forms of ESP that we can experience in dreams or while awake. What of a dream that reveals facts to us that are unknown to everyone else (i.e., clairvoyance)? This cannot be a matter of receiving a thought impression if there is no one sending that thought. Or, what of a prophetic dream (i.e., precognition)? Again, the mechanism that helped us understand telepathy does not seem to apply.

These possible instances of ESP suggest an alternative

process for psychic experience. The theory in the readings is that we can attune ourselves to the superconscious mind and thereby obtain (1) information unknown to any other human consciousness or (2) information about likely future events. In other words the psychic mechanism is at least two-fold. We can go within ourselves to the source of infinite knowledge for *any* type of psychic experience; or in the case of telepathy, our awareness can merely "reach out" to contact the thought forms being created by others.

By whatever pathway we experience ESP, the principle of oneness is the foundation. No doubt many books could be written on the meaning of just this concept. The entire philosophy and psychology of living from the Cayce readings rests on this very assumption. A way of understanding oneness is to say that all of life is interrelated. Rather than view the universe as fragments and seek to understand how they might influence and affect each other, we might do better to begin with a notion of oneness—the essential unity of the universe—and watch how the events we observe reflect that unity.

It is interesting to note that in recent years many branches of science have moved in this direction. Astrophysicists speak of a "big bang theory" suggesting that the universe began from a common origin billions of years ago and that the movements of the galaxies and the stars can be traced to a common, unifying history. Ecologists have begun to view the events on our planet from a perspective of oneness. They realize that there is a far deeper kind of interrelatedness to life on our earth than we may previously have recognized.

Cayce's readings also speak of oneness in a vareity of ways. Sometimes it is in terms of the oneness of all force. That is, the universe is made up of one essential energy which can express itself in many ways. Electricity and the energy you feel when you get angry are merely two expressions of one fundamental energy. This is an extremely important notion to our spiritual growth because it implies that growth in consciousness is merely a matter of transforming the way in which we use energy. If there were an "anger energy" and a "love energy," the growth might involve suppressing "anger energy." However, because of the essential oneness of all force, it becomes a matter of transforming rather than suppressing life in order to change.

At other times the readings speak of the oneness of minds. At the superconscious level of mind there is a quality of oneness and essential interrelatedness. And at the subconscious level as well there is a quality of oneness which allows an individual to be sensitive to the thought form images of another.

A third perspective of oneness is the relationship of body, mind and soul. This point of view is rapidly gaining popularity in the professional world, especially in what is termed "holistic medicine." Edgar Cayce's medical readings could be seen as pioneer work in holistic medicine. He adhered closely to the notion that any physically therapeutic procedure should be accompanied with a proper mental attitude and spiritual purpose. It is the simultaneous convergence of the three that makes a treatment holistic, a fact that unfortunately is missed by many. Balanced living is not necessarily holistic. For example, if you watch a violent television show while you eat organic food, you do not "balance" the detrimental effect of the mental state on digestion by meditating later in the day. If our living has to totally reflect a belief in the essential oneness of body, mind and soul, then we would attend to our attitudes and ideals as we carry out each action of daily life.

There is a difference between body, mind and soul merely affecting each other and the three actually being one. The difference is described in this passage from the present writer's book *Experiments in A Search for God.*

What does it mean when we say that the body, mind, and soul are one? One possibility is that there are three separate structures that are very closely related to each other—the activities of one directly affecting the other two. This is illustrated in the following diagram:

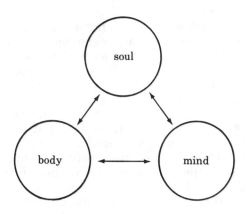

Practitioners of psychosomatic medicine would support at least a portion of this model (perhaps denying the soul), because it conceptualizes two independent structures that have a direct effect on each other.

However, this is really not a *oneness*. We might come closer to an accurate model of oneness in the following diagram:

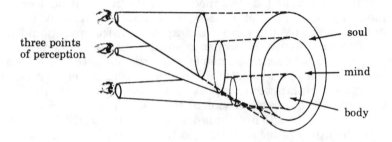

three points of perception

soul

mind

body

In this model we find that the body is an expression of a portion of what has been created mentally (i.e., a concrete, materialized thought form). And the mental activity of an individual is one aspect of the many potentialities of the soul. We have not so much three autonomous systems, but a oneness. We conceptualize three parts because our three-dimensional consciousness leads us to see the oneness from three points of perception. (*Experiments in A Search for God,* pp. 126, 127)

The reader might well wonder by now what all this discussion of oneness actually has to do with dreams. To answer this we might re-list these three perspectives of oneness from the Cayce readings and include the insight about dreams which this may provide.

(1) The oneness of all force. In other words, any expression of energy can be *transformed* to another expression which is more in keeping with our ideals. This means that the images we see in dreams—no matter how distasteful or discouraging they may seem—do not need to be suppressed. The energy that goes into their make-up simply needs to be lifted.

(2) The oneness of all mind. The mental structure of each indiviudal is so created that there is a natural avenue for psychic communication. That avenue is especially opened to us when we are not focused on the confines of normal waking consciousness. A dream of telepathic communication is not a freakish experience but instead one which we might come to expect when we recognize the essential unity of higher levels of mind.

(3) The oneness of body, mind and soul. This principle will be important when we explore dreams related to the physical body, in a later chapter. However, it also provides a significant insight for ESP dreams. It suggests that sometimes our psychic dreams are best interpreted in a way that reflects another

aspect of the triad (e.g., the body representing the mental state). Consider the following example. A man dreamed that he watched a close friend fall down a flight of stairs and hurt herself. In subsequent weeks he saw that the dream had been precognitive. However, the woman did not experience a physical injury as depicted in the dream. Instead, she went through a period of mental stress and was emotionally down. It was not that the man's dream had been inaccurate but merely that it had depicted the essential oneness of her body, mind and soul. Perhaps at the deeper level of consciousness in which the dream occurred there was not clarity concerning the level at which the difficulty would manifest. Whatever the case, the principle of oneness should encourage us to look at potential psychic dreams with an eye toward this kind of altered meaning.

Finally, in our overall consideration of psychic ability, the question remains, "What is the best source of psychic information?" Not surprisingly, the Cayce readings suggest that it is the individual himself, through an attunement to the superconscious. Even though it may seem especially attractive to go to a reputed professional psychic for answers, we can learn to give our own readings for ourselves. Particularly through our dreams we can discover this potential to obtain answers to our questions.

One woman who received readings from Edgar Cayce brought him a dream in which she seemed to be giving a reading herself (136-72). Although no specific questions were answered in this particular dream, she did experience what it was like to go through the suggestive procedure used by Cayce at the beginning of each reading. When she questioned the validity of the dream experience in the subsequent reading by Cayce himself, she was told that she had attained the same condition he entered for giving his readings. (136-72, A-2)

In another illustration, a man gave himself a reading through a dream. Interestingly, he had been trying to get a reading from a well-known psychic, but things did not seem to be working out. He had written to the psychic, enclosing his questions, but had not had a response. Then he had this dream:

Dreamed that I received a letter from the psychic explaining that he couldn't give me a reading and that I should get one from someone else. I cannot remember that name. He says that this other one is just as good. The letter went on to suggest that I analyze SELF, that I take the next two weeks and dedicate them to working out the small things that are often overlooked about self—greeting friends and neighbors, everyone, with a smile, extending a helping hand, etc. I felt disappointed not to be getting a reading, but the letter surmised my feelings and added that everyone must meet their own karma. (Later in waking life I called this psychic and discovered that the reading had been canceled. A letter had been sent saying that the reading had been canceled but it went to the wrong address and hadn't arrived.)

Examples of Oneness in Dreams

Our understanding of oneness is, of course, not limited to dreams of a psychic nature. However, such dreams do provide us with especially good illustrations of how the oneness of all force and oneness of all minds can directly affect our experiences. In the case of some dreams cited in this chapter, it is difficult to determine precisely what form of ESP is being demonstrated. Frequently there is a mixture in the dream of telepathic content (i.e., things known by another human mind) and clairvoyant content (i.e., things unknown to any other human mind). In addition, there may be elements of a precognitive nature—that is, a warning about likely future events.

All three of these are found in a series of dreams that a man had about his mother and her health. Two of the dreams are as follows:

Q-1. [900], Friday morning, Feb. 4, 1927. Saw my mother in a faint. Conditions seemed abnormal. I decided to take things in hand and started to massage her from feet up and also to give her osteopathic treatment. 900-300

Q-4. Saw my mother sick upon her return from her trip. I said: "Oh, yes, she has Fleisher's or Fisher's disease. [Fleischner's or Fiedler's disease?] I had the same thing— remember?" (This referring to time I had German measles and yellow jaundice.) Then turning to my mother I said: "Had you taken the osteopath treatments as you were told to, this would never have happened." Then I thought that maybe her sickness would convince Ma—yet reasoned that it might not in spite of all. 900-343

Cayce's interpretation of the first dream suggests that there is a combination of clairvoyance and precognition. Through a oneness of all force the subconscious mind of the dreamer was able to perceive conditions in the material world that were unknown to others. In this case we assume that even the mother did not fully recognize her physical condition. The dream also has an implied precognitive element. Perhaps from the dream's perspective there is more of a oneness of time and the dream is able to "see" into what the future is likely to bring. In this example the future is likely to be more severe physical problems if preventive action is not taken. The essence of Cayce's interpretation of the first dream states: "So, being forewarned, be forearmed—and, as has been given, insist that such is carried out to prevent the occurrence of such conditions." (900-300)

In the second dream there is the combination of telepathic and clairvoyant influences. Cayce's interpretation indicates that not only has the dreamer correctly perceived a need of the mother's body (i.e., for osteopathic adjustments), but he has also telepathically picked up her attitude. In the last line of the dream, he realizes that she will probably continue to be unconvinced about the need for more careful attention to health procedures. Of course, the real interpretation of this dream is far more than just saying it is a telepathic and clairvoyant experience. The reading given on the dream strongly urges the dreamer to take this information he has psychically received in his dream and to insist on the physical treatment despite the mother's attitude.

In another example from the Cayce dream readings, it is primarily telepathy that is involved in the experience. One man—who in the readings was assigned the number 195—had been working on the design of an airplane that would incorporate a gyroscopic principle in the motor. A friend—number 900—then had a remarkable dream in which he viewed in detail the plans that his friend had been developing for the airplane. Apparently the dreamer had never had the opportunity to see firsthand any information about the proposed airplane, yet he telepathically perceived what had been going on in the inventor's mind. The reading given on this dream says:

Now we have many varied conditions as to how this may be approached. To the one—[900]—this [is] that [indication] of two forces in activity: The ability of the inner self [900] to vision, in that as may be called telepathic manner that [which] as is of the interpretation of a mental activity of [195]—which is, as has been given, that [indication of how] "Thoughts are Deeds."

195-59

What is it that stimulates such remarkable instances of ESP? The oneness is always there and yet not all of our dreams seem to be of a psychic nature. What are the factors that influence the subconscious mind to make use of the oneness of all force and of all minds in order to produce a psychic dream?

Although there may be other factors, the Cayce readings suggest at least two. First is the matter of our personal concerns. We are more likely to have a dream with psychic content about some condition if we have a sense of needing that information. One passage from the readings put it quite bluntly. Consciousness in the dream state will be "directed toward those conditions in which the body-conscious is so wrapped-up." (900-314, A-1) Nevertheless, this is not an exclusive factor. Even when we are extremely concerned about some matter in waking life, we may fail to have a psychic dream about it. We may block the dream for other psychological reasons, or our ideals and purposes may not be proper. Similarly, we may occasionally have a psychic dream about something that we had not consciously been concerned with. However, despite these qualifications, our conscious concerns will be seen to be one key factor in stimulating a dream involving ESP.

A second factor is the *quality* of our concern. The selfless desire to serve others will especially enhance the likelihood of a psychic dream. This should not surprise us. Is not a desire to serve others an expression of the inherent oneness of all life? It should not be surprising then that a mind consciously directed by oneness would have opened to it the psychic channels of oneness. We can expect such dreams when we "seek to satisfy that desire, or that love intent toward [another]." (137-53)

All this is to say that there is an ambivalent nature to time as we see it. What may seem like a prediction about the future may really be a statement to us saying, "Here is what is likely to happen if current conditions are allowed to proceed on their current track." This view of precognitive dreams offers us the possibility of using our free will to intervene if the dream seems to be a warning. Free will is an essential element of our growth in awareness and without it we might fall into a fatalistic notion of precognitive dreams, saying that our dreams have shown us something that is fated to be. Of course, some precognitive dreams will not be warning dreams but instead encouraging ones. They may show us the eventual fruits of present efforts that to our physical perception do not seem to be bringing positive results yet.

As a final note on the nature of precognitive dreams, they offer us a possible explanation of the "déja vu" experience, in which a person feels that he has already experienced something going on at that moment. Might it be that we dream the events of daily life weeks, or even years, before they happen? Perhaps we usually do not recall such dreams and it is only when the event happens that it stimulates a vague kind of recall. In the words of one reading: " ... for any condition ever becoming a reality is first dreamed." (136-7)

Examples of Precognitive Dreams

A man once brought to Edgar Cayce a dream in which he and his brother were in a dark room. They viewed the coffins of three dead relatives: their father, grandfather and uncle. However, in the dream he realized that this was strange, because when last he heard his uncle was still alive. Cayce's interpretation was brief, simply stating that this dream showed the fact that the uncle would soon die. (900-240) There is no indication that this is a warning dream, for that would imply that perhaps the dreamer should do something to avert the conditions shown. Instead the dream seems to be merely a statement of fact—something presented to the dreamer because he cared about his uncle and could perhaps ease the uncle's transition through prayer or other forms of support.

In a later experience, the same dreamer brought to Cayce a dream of traveling in Europe with his family. The comments in the reading gave the following explanation: " . . . There is projected into the entity's vision those conditions which are, in two years, to come to pass in the entity's life, see?" (900-259) Is this reading suggesting that anytime we dream of traveling in a foreign country it is predictive of a trip there? Undoubtedly this is not the case. It is certainly not an easy matter to recognize a psychic dream and this problem will be addressed at the end of the chapter. However, in this instance the lesson seems to be that we should consider precognition as a possible interpretation of a dream of traveling to a new place. The dream may stimulate us to think about (1) what it would be like to visit that place or (2) the ideals and purposes we might have if we were to travel there. At the very least such a self-examination is likely to lead to somewhat greater self-understanding.

In another example, of a personal nature, the elusive character of time itself is demonstrated. We might ask ourselves how far into the future we imagine it is possible to dream of an event *in detail?* A week? A month? I had suspected that this might be the limits of detailed precognitive experiences. Certainly prediction of a broader scope such as natural cataclysms might be already set in motion years before they occurred; but as for *specific* personal experience I suspected that the time differential was much briefer.

125

My attitude was quickly changed upon hearing the following story. I had just completed a call-in radio show for a midwest metropolitan station. The talk show hostess stopped me on the way out to share a precognitive dream she had had many years ago. She related that as a child she had dreamed of being older and going on a date with a young man. At the time of the dream she did not recognize him. They parked near a lake in his new car and were kissing when a mongoloid girl crawled up onto the hood of the car and peeked in through the windshield. The young man got out of the car to try to get her to leave. In the ensuing events the mongoloid girl inadvertently fell in the lake. The couple then sped off to get away and were subsequently stopped by a policeman for speeding. Several years after this dream she met a young man who resembled the dream character; and *eleven years* after the dream, the events of the dream actually happened! However, in this case she did not let the man get out of the car, fearing what might happen to the girl. As in the dream they left the scene in a hurry and were stopped for speeding. To me it seemed quite remarkable that a dream could be so accurately predictive in details eleven years in advance. It renewed my sense of humility and respect for the laws of time, space and mind which I so little understood.

The Warning Dream

Probably the most practical type of precognitive dream is the one that warns us and gives us a chance to alter the course of events. The dream theory of the Cayce readings is so strong on this matter as to suggest that we all have warnings and presumably these come most often through our dreams. "There are *no* individuals who haven't at *some* time been warned as respecting that that may arise in their daily or physical experience!" (5754-3)

These warnings can be of a wide variety. Warnings about health conditions are likely for most individuals, and they will be exmained closely in a later chapter on dreams pertaining to the physical body. Since the man who received by far the most dream readings from Cayce was a businessman, we are not surprised to find many examples of warnings about business concerns. A physician might expect an equal number of warning dreams about his practice; a mother, warning dreams about her children.

One of the most practical uses of a warning dream is in the decision making process. Instead of passively waiting, hoping for a warning dream about something soon to go wrong, we can use more initiative. When we face a decision we should pose the question so that it can be answered yes or no. Then we should take into account all the factors we consciously know and make the best possible decision we can. It should also measure up well to our chosen spiritual ideal.

Actually this conscious decision is a tentative one. We are saying, "According to the best I know, this is what I intend to do." Then after a period of attunement through meditation we should ask the question again, and listen within for a confirmation or denial of what we have already chosen on a tentative basis.

Some people receive an intuitive response from the inner self immediately. However, many find the response in a dream. Rather than answer the question directly the dream is precognitive; it shows what is likely to occur in the future *if the dreamer follows the course on which he has tentatively decided.* Based on what he sees in this precognitive dream he can decide more effectively if this is the best choice.

Symbolism and Alternations in Psychic Dreams

We may be more likely to recognize a psychic dream if we realize some of the qualifications for how ESP works in the dream state. Although some of our dreams may quite *literally* depict psychic information, others will clothe the message in the symbols of the dream. Often in interpreting a dream Cayce would make a comment such as "These may be seen in conditions about to come to pass, see? Not as literal—these as emblematical, see?" (294-36) In other words, we may have a precognitive dream which is presented in a symbolic way. The same holds true for telepathic and clairvoyant dreams.

For example, many people have dreamed of catastrophies such as hurricanes and earthquakes. Such dreams could be literally predictive; but when such events do not happen, we are left to conclude that the precognitive nature of the dream may have related to the dreamer himself. Perhaps it was suggestive of a sudden and destructive change in the dreamer's own life or the life of another of close relation.

Similarly, what appears to be an ordinary dream may actually include instances of ESP. We should be alert for possible psychic communication whenever we dream of someone we know. Even if the dream may be interpreted solely in terms of the dreamer's own life, it may also contain psychic information. We should be prepared to act on *both* possible applications of the dream.

To illustrate how a relatively ordinary dream might be seen as a kind of psychic perception, consider the following instance. This dream was brought to Edgar Cayce for a reading:

Q-4. Then I was in temple listening to a sermon. I started to change my clothes as I sat in my pew. Taking off my pants and sitting in my BVDs I attracted the attention of some people in a back pew to my left who were laughing at me and making fun of me. They grew so loud and boisterous in their abuse that the usher came up to them to make them keep quiet. They pointed me out to the one in authority and he looked at me in disgusted fashion, but held his peace and told the mockers to keep quiet. Meanwhile I was struggling to get my new or other pants on, feeling embarrassed. At last I succeeded, but felt foolish and most looked at me with either aversion or scorn or sarcasm.

900-202

Cayce's commenatry indicates that this is a precognitive dream showing changes that the dreamer will be making in thought and action concerning theology. In making these changes he will draw attention to himself and may experience ridicule by others. This interpretative approach is a good example of isolating the theme of the dream and applying it to the future.

The dream may also slightly alter psychic information in its presentation. In this case it is not so much a matter of symbolic portrayal of the message, but only a distortion or alteration. An excellent example of this process is shown in the experience of a businessman in Virginia Beach. He dreamed one night that an appointment for the next morning had been canceled due to a snowstorm in Virginia Beach. The person who was to come telephoned and said that he and his friend from New York could not make it across town in the snow. When he awoke the next morning the weather was fine: no snow. However, upon reaching the office he received a call from the same man who had called in the dream. In this case the man announced that he would have to cancel the appointment because his friend from New York had not yet arrived. There had just been a snowstorm *in New York* and she had missed her plane flight to Virginia Beach.

One theme of the dream proved to be accurate: an appointment is canceled due to snow. However, the psychic nature of the dream is somewhat altered from the way things turned out. It may be that dreams often act in a *parsimonious* fashion, stating things as succinctly as possible. This may seem like an unusual statement in light of some of our long, jumbled dreams; however, this example illustrates a process that can often be observed through dream study. Rather than introduce two characters a dream will often simply merge one into the other at some point in the story. Rather than introduce a second setting (i.e., New York) this dream merely combined the condition of snow with the setting already being used. We should be prepared for this principle of parsimony in looking for ESP in our dreams. There may be a slight alteration or distortion of the information merely because it was simpler to say things that way.

Recognizing a Psychic Dream

Identifying a dream which incorporates ESP is not an easy task. It may well be that most, if not all, of our dreams have some degree of psychic ability involved in their formation. The problem is to recognize those dreams which offer practical guidance for daily living.

Although it is by no means a foolproof procedure, a three-step process is suggested for finding dreams which make use of the law of oneness and which psychically perceive needed information. In most instances it will be advisable to use this three-step procedure in conjunction with other dream interpretation approaches. It is an exciting possibility that any given dream may contain evidence for ESP. However, if we go to the extreme of thinking every dream is telepathy, clairvoyance or precognition, then we will miss many insights from our dream which do not fit this category. Therefore, the reader is strongly encouraged to apply the search for psychic dreams along with the other interpretative approaches already described. Briefly the three steps are as follows:

1. Adopt an openminded attitude toward ESP in dreams. It is a well-documented fact that persons who are open to the possibility of psychic ability do better on ESP tests. In working with our dreams it is suggested that we constantly be alert for evidence of ESP. We can do this by asking ourselves simple questions about the dream. For example, "If this dream were telepathic, what would it be telling me about the dream characters?" Or, "If this were a warning dream, what might it be warning me of?"

This step does not involve any profound insight with psychic dreams and may at first seem rather simplistic. However, understanding usually begins with openness and it is such an attitude we must foster. It is probably wise, in addition, to cultivate an appreciation for ESP dreams by examining those we have had months or years earlier. Often it takes that long to realize that a particular dream actually contained evidence for ESP.

2. Imagine that a particular dream is psychically derived and determine a constructive application. In this step we are proceeding only hypothetically. We in effect ask, "*If* this dream were influenced by ESP, how would I apply it in a way that corresponds to my ideal?" If we cannot find an answer to this question, we are probably better off to pursue another line of interpretative approach for that particular dream. For example, some people have dreams which they feel are precognitive, but the only way they can imagine to react to them is with anxiety. Others have dreams which seem telepathic concerning another, but the only way they can imagine using them is to subtly get the upper hand in the relationship. In these instances it is best to stop the procedure here at step two and approach things from another angle.

Despite this potential problem, we will often be able to determine a constructive way the dream might be applied. Perhaps this would be a healing action that may alter a difficult condition which has been warned of. Or it may be a loving response to a person we dreamed about. Remember that step two is still only hypothetical—we do not know yet whether or not the dream really is ESP, but only imagine how we might constructively apply it if this were the case. When we find a suitable solution at this stage, we are ready for step three.

3. Apply the response determined in step two and observe the results. In this way we get feedback—we learn. Although it is not always easy to judge results, with persistent application we will begin to learn when the dream was actually using ESP. We discover inner "cues" that tip us off. Some people have found that a valid ESP dream almost always includes a particular quality: a specific person, a certain feeling upon awakening, a distinct type of story line, etc. It is a personal kind of thing and each person must discover it for himself. That discovery comes only by completing all three steps *many times.* Just sitting and asking "Could this be a warning dream?" will never teach us how to recognize an ESP experience. There is no substitute for getting out and *trying* the constructive responses we see in potential psychic dreams. We may make some mistakes and assume some dreams are ESP when they are not. But our safeguard is that we can go through this learning process by selectively acting only on responses that would be in keeping with our ideals anyway.

Summary

The principle of oneness gives us the key to understanding how a psychic dream can happen. This principle can be applied to time to produce precognition; to space to produce clairvoyance; and to the oneness of all minds to produce telepathy. Working with our dreams we discover that the best psychic source is within ourselves. Through proper attunement we may begin to give ourselves "readings" much as Cayce did for others.

Two of the most significant factors in psychic dreams are the concerns we consciously entertain and the degree of our love and purposefulness toward that concern. However, we should not assume that all of our dreams are best interpreted as precognition, clairvoyance or telepathy. There are certain steps which have been outlined and they can be useful in developing an ability to recognize ESP in dreams. As we repeatedly use these steps we may learn what internal cues or qualities of our dreams signal a likely psychic experience.

Exercises in Application

1. Use the decision making exercise in conjunction with studying your dreams. Use the following steps:
   1) Set the spiritual ideal as to purposes.
   2) Pose the question so that it may be answered by a Yes or No.
   3) Make a rational logical decision, Yes or No.
   4) Measure the decision by the ideal.
   5) Before going to bed, meditate—not on the question but for attunement.
   6) Ask in silence, Yes or No. Listen! Then observe your dreams for the following few days for feedback. Dreams will likely show you the consequences or results of following the tentative decision you made in step number three above.
   7) Measure the final decision by the ideal.
   8) Act on the decision.
If you are in a group, allow each member to briefly share his or her experience with this exercise.

2. Choose a dream which you feel might have evidence of ESP and complete the following flow chart of steps. If you are in a group, share your experiences in applying this exercise.

Looking for an ESP Dream

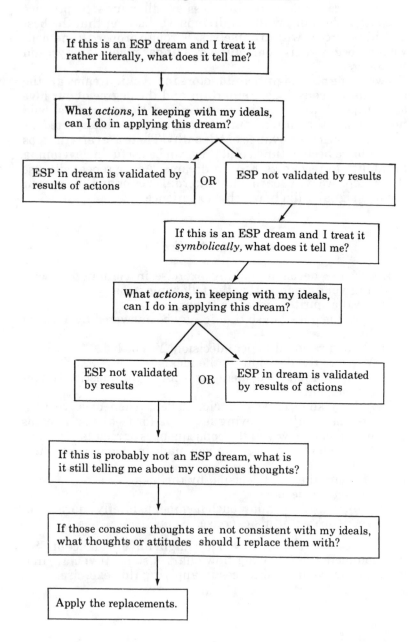

If this is an ESP dream and I treat it rather literally, what does it tell me?

↓

What *actions,* in keeping with my ideals, can I do in applying this dream?

ESP in dream is validated by results of actions

OR

ESP not validated by results

If this is an ESP dream and I treat it *symbolically,* what does it tell me?

What *actions,* in keeping with my ideals, can I do in applying this dream?

ESP not validated by results

OR

ESP in dream is validated by results of actions

If this is probably not an ESP dream, what is it still telling me about my conscious thoughts?

If those conscious thoughts are not consistent with my ideals, what thoughts or attitudes should I replace them with?

Apply the replacements.

Chapter Ten
THE OPPORTUNITY IN DREAMING

In an earlier chapter we observed how the dimension of patience is the key to our understanding of life experiences in time and space. This concept is an aspect of Cayce's three-dimensional notion of physical life.

We also noted that both time and space could be broken into three sub-dimensions or sub-measurements. For time we have past, present and future; for space we have height, width and depth. Might not we also expect that patience, as a dimension, also contains three sub-divisions? The breakdown is not explicitly found in the readings, but the concepts are. This writer discovered, through a series of his own dreams, that three sub-dimensions of patience could be an especially helpful principle.

Three progressive measurements or stages of patience are passive waiting, acceptance and thankfulness. In other words, there are at least three distinct perspectives of patience and they constitute a growth sequence. Each step along that sequence represents greater understanding of the meaning and purpose of our experiences in time and space.

The most simplistic notion of patience is merely waiting for something to happen. Often this is a matter of grudgingly putting up with things because there is some type of payoff later. For example, it is a kind of patience to wait in line at the bank to get your paycheck cashed. You may passively put up with there being a long line or you may be irritated by it. However, in this first perspective of patience the very fact that you do stand in line—that you do wait—demonstrates a simple form of patience. What is important at this stage is your *action* and not your inner attitude and feeling about what is going on. Frequently that inner state is not very positive.

The initial *development* in patience is to work on your feelings and attitudes as you go through the action of waiting or any other life experience. So the second stage can be called acceptance. In this case our attitudes and feelings are not necessarily constructive, but at least we have turned off the resentment or irritation. A person standing in line at the bank might replace his irritation with thoughts of daily life concerns. That is, he has accepted the current state of affairs and has found a way to wait in line with his mind in at least a neutral state.

Beyond this, another development is possible. As a person meets physical life events and has turned off thoughts and feelings such as irritation, he can then be *thankful* for the situation. He can see the current conditions as an *opportunity* to express his ideals. In our example of the man in the bank, he may choose to pray for the people in line with him or strike up a conversation with one of them. At this third stage or sub-dimension there is the potential fulfillment and mastery of the dimension of patience. It comes as we realize the meaning of opportunity. Our lives begin to change as we meet each experience with an attitude of "Thank you for this opportunity."

Another way of understanding opportunity is that things happen to us because they provide the chance for the event to stimulate something in us. The Eastern notion of karma provides a good example. Whether or not you personally accept the theory of reincarnation (i.e., that a soul returns in other lives in human form), the problem posed by karma is illustrative of how opportunity works. When something troublesome happens to us, how do we respond? A person who believes in reincarnation might say that this is the law of karma at work—in a previous life he probably did something that has resulted in the present difficulty.

However, in a sense, this implies a punitive God. It pictures the universe as being run by an intelligence that keeps careful records and unswervingly hands out punishment when it is due. In this view of the universe we might ask, "Where do grace and forgiveness come in?" Perhaps what is needed is another intrepretation of the law of karma, one that includes our understanding of patience and opportunity.

We might begin to see that karmic situations happen to us, not because God is punishing us for what we have earned, but because out of God's grace we are given the *opportunity* to react differently and break an old cycle of cause-and-effect. When we say "thank you" within ourselves to even the most burdensome situation, we are now in a position to seize the opportunity before us: to respond with love and to heal karmic patterns within our souls.

This very process of oportunity is frequently presented in our dreams. Just as waking life events give us opportunities, so do dream events. This can happen in at least two broad categories of dream experience.

First, a dream can be an opportunity to directly awaken something in us. That is to say, many times the message of a dream is not hidden. It is rather the direct experience which the dream provides. How often we may miss this in our efforts to apply sophisticated interpretative approaches! Sometimes the dream presents an elaborate story merely as an opportunity to stimulate a lesson, attitude or feeling in us. In such cases it is not necessary to know the details of symbology or elaborate tricks for ferreting out hidden meanings. Instead it is a matter of recognizing how the events of the dream present the chance for us to see things or respond to things in a new way.

For example, we might ask ourselves this question in studying a dream: "If this had been a waking life experience, what *lesson* would I have learned?" A young woman brought a dream (140-10, Q-1) to Cayce in which she was leaving a restaurant with her husband. She was driving their new car and started down a lakeside road. Suddenly she seemed to go over the edge of the embankment. The car stopped and she thought she had time to put on the emergency brake, holding it long enough so they could escape, but instead she did nothing. Finally she jumped from the car and into the lake. The car fell after her and on top of her, and it killed her. The commentary from the reading indicates that this is not a warning dream about a specific event but instead it is a lesson. The dream came as an opportunity to awaken in her this awareness: we must act when we can on what we know to do.

... That is, then: To know to do good and do it not, to him it is imputed as sin. **This lesson is manifested to the entity here. Use it. No special significance as to a given time, place or condition, but as relates to Life, see?** 140-10

No special knowledge of symbology is required to understand this dream. Perhaps at one level of interpretation there is a reason why her husband, the car and the lake were used in the story. However, the essential message is that an opportunity has been presented: to do what she knows to do. Even though she missed the opportunity in the dream, the lesson has been awakened. If she can apply the lesson in waking life, the purpose of the dream will have been fulfilled.

In another example a man dreamed that he was talking with a friend. He told the friend that he was giving all his profits from land investments to a certain charitable cause. In response the dreamer received criticism and ridicule. His brother appeared in the dream and found fault with him for having divulged his intentions. At first the dreamer claimed he could not help it, then realized that it would have been best if he had not said these things to his friend (900-376, Q-3)

Cayce's interpretation is an answer to the question, "If this had been a waking life experience, what lesson would I have learned?" The answer is simply not to brag about the good one intends to do. In the words of the actual reading:

. . . **Even again, as has been given, let not thy good be evilspoken of through any effort of thine self to appear above the ordinary individual. Let rather what would be said, concerning good deeds from any source, come from others than from self.** 900-376

There is a second question we can pose to ourselves to identify a dream which directly awakens something. It asks, "What is the *attitude* which this dream gives me the opportunity to awaken?" In other words, we assume that for some dreams the elaborate story line is a carefully constructed situation which is likely to stimulate a needed attitude.

This approach is used on a dream from the same individual as the last example. In the experience (900-288, Q-1) he came to the Cayce house, apparently wanting to share some new spiritual insight or gain approval for his latest understanding of truth. He found that Cayce was sick and had apparently been drinking more alcohol than was good for him. He was being attended by a doctor who announced his general disbelief in the value of psychic readings. The dreamer felt alone. The one person from whom he was sure he could find approval and support had turned out to be not applying his own teachings.

The interpretation given indicates that this has nothing to do with Cayce himself but instead was a dream story created to stimulate a particular attitude in the dreamer—namely, that no matter what others may do, he knows the truth and proper way of living. The dream awakened a state of mind which allowed the dreamer to find an inner source of approval without needing confirmation by someone else.

This approach to discovering opportunities in our dreams is further illustrated by this experience. A man dreamed that he was at his office and his supervisor came in to see him. The supervisor began to compliment him about what a good job he was doing. Naturally this made the dreamer feel very good about himself. He realized how worth while and helpful it was to have someone think highly of what you have done.

The answer is clear if the dreamer asks himself in studying the experience, "What is the attitude which this dream gives me the opportunity to awaken?" Although the experience provides the opportunity to feel good, more importantly it stimulates an attitude of wanting to compliment others on their own work. His dream has awakened him to recognition of how healing this can be. However, just realizing this is not enough. The dream is fully interpreted only as he follows through and actually compliments fellow workers as a service to them.

Finally we can pose a question of our dream that parallels the one of attitude: "What is the *feeling* which the dream gives me the opportunity to experience?" A man dreamed that he had knocked out his wife and she had become unconscious. Then he became remorseful and taking her in his arms called her to come to. But the injury had been too much for her and it appeared that she might die. He awoke with great feelings of regret. (900-246, Q-1, 2)

Cayce's interpretation suggests that this dream was not precognitive of harm about to come to the wife. Instead it was simply an opportunity presented to stimulate a particular feeling—not regret, but deeper appreciation and more attention to his wife.

In summary, the first category of dream opportunity relates to the direct awakening of a lesson, an attitude or a feeling. We can pose simple questions to ourselves about any dream which may help to identify this category of opportunity. Of course, merely awakening a lesson, attitude or feeling is not enough. The purpose of the dream is fulfilled only as there is a subsequent application in daily life.

Opportunities to Discover Talents

A second category of dream opportunity relates to the discovery of talents. Latent within us all are abilities which we have denied or simply never knew were there. Dreams can present situations in which we experience these talents. These experiences are opportunities to expand the boundaries of our self-concept. When applied they become a type of vocational guide for some people, or a direction to a richer life experience for others.

There are several examples from the Cayce readings of talent opportunities. In one instance, a man dreamed that he was helping someone who was sick to her stomach. He took her to a drugstore where he mixed a solution of three ingredients. Upon drinking it the woman went outside and vomited. The dreamer felt sure that this would be good for her condition. Cayce's comments on the dream (900-319, A-4) suggest that this experience was to illustrate that the dreamer had a latent talent to help people in a physical way. It indicated that a personal study of anatomy, along with the work he was already doing with the Cayce physical readings, would enhance his ability as a helper.

In another example the same dreamer reported this experience: "Saw the huge concrete bridge the C.R.R. of N.J. is building, especially the wonderful $10,000,000.00 foundation." (900-112, Q-1)

At first glance this does not seem to indicate any latent talent, unless we want to guess that perhaps the dreamer could be a good bridge builder (either literally or in a symbolic way). The reading given on the dream, however, focused on the magnitude of the project in the dream. It suggests that the dreamer is capable of coping with far-reaching projects, provided the foundation or purpose is correct. The reading says, " . . . those illustrations of the stupendous work the body physically and mentally [is] capable of coping with and the necessity of a firm and fixed foundation . . . " (900-112, A-1)

In another illustration, not from the readings, a woman who was in *A Search for God* Study Group reported:

> I dreamed I was working (at the A.R.E.). A man called and spoke very softly. He was disturbed and needed to talk. He said he wanted to murder an employee of his. I told him to come over and talk. It was 4:00 P.M. when he came, and I had trouble finding a quiet place to talk with him. There were people sitting and talking in an area I needed to use. I felt a bit frustrated and finally asked them to leave, and they just got up and left.

Her Study Group worked with her on several possible interpretations. One approach was to see this as a latent talent: her ability to be a counselor to those who had problems they were ashamed of. The dreamer already knew she was a good and sensitive listener; however, she was not applying it in a systematic way. The dream also seems to show that she will need to be rather assertive in order to have the chance to apply this helping ability. However, as the dream illustrates (i.e., asking the others to leave), she does have the ability to do this, too.

A final perspective of the opportunity to recognize talents concerns reincarnation. The readings support the theory of reincarnation and indicate that dreams can show us talents we have developed in past lives. One woman was told that in the development of her writing career she could draw upon dream images of past life conditions. These dreams could form the background for her writing efforts in the present.

As to the appearances in the earth—these find expression more in what is called the senses, or the physical dreams. For the entity does dream, oft. It should record more often the experiences. These kept or paralleled or drawn upon for the basis of expressions as may be given in the abilities as the writer, may be of great value to the entity in a material, in a mental and spiritual way.

Then in the name of Cassie Eversole, the entity was active in home building; being an instructor or teacher in the groups organized in that vicinity during the period. There the entity gained, and yet its dreams of places and conditions may at present form the background of those talents or abilities for the entity to give expression to same.   3135-1

Another woman was told in her reading that in a past life she had developed a talent for putting to practicel use various metals and minerals. When questioned as to how she would be able to re-awaken that ability, the readings answered that the knowledge could be obtained in dreams. (993-2, A-16)

In summary, a promising category of dream opportunities is the discovery of latent talents. The examples have shown that it is not always easy to recognize such dreams. Even though some may be so direct as to show us doing exactly what that talent is, others will be presented more symbolically (e.g., the huge bridge dream). In order to identify these dreams we must keep an open, playful attitude. We should be willing to question ourselves about the individual aspects of a dream, asking, "Does this show me that I am capable of doing something I did not know I could?" If we have developed too rigid a notion of what we can and cannot do we are likely to miss such valuable opportunities to expand the horizons of our lives.

Exercises in Application

Examine a dream for evidence of opportunities being offered. Imagine that the dream had been a waking life experience. What lesson would you have learned? What feelings or attitudes were awakened? Make a list of your answers to these questions. Then examine the dream for evidence of an opportunity to discover a talent or ability.

If you are unable to find dream opportunities in the first example, try other dreams until you find one. Once you have, write out a short statement of how you could begin to *apply* that lesson, attitude, feeling or talent in daily life. Simply decide what the *first step* in application would be, and then do it.

If you are in a group working with dreams share your experiences with this exercise after you have made some efforts at applying what you have written down.

Chapter Eleven
DAY AND NIGHT: BALANCE
THROUGH COMPENSATION

Knowing the essential oneness of all force we can understand the seeming opposites of life to be actually polarities. This distinction is crucial if we are to have the prospect of harmonious living. Whereas opposites are continually warring with each other, polarities within a unity are a creative tension. Through our dreams there is a work being done to optimize the possibilites of these creative interactions.

What do we mean by polarities? They are conditions that we all experience. They are influences that seem to pull us in contradictory ways. For example, the qualities of masculine and feminine are polarities within the soul, which is of neither gender but manifests as one or the other in materiality. Carl Jung has pointed out that within each woman there is the pattern of her masculine nature, which he called the animus. Similarly, within the psyche of a man there is the feminine counterpart of his soul, the anima. These parts of oneself can be depicted in dreams by the universal or archetypal symbol of a character of the opposite sex. For a more careful study of the animus and anima, the reader is encouraged to examine Jung's excellent essay "Marriage as a Psychological Relationship" found in his published *Collective Works*.

What is most significant in our exploration of polarities is that the masculine and feminine influences within us are not irreconcilable opposites but rather aspects of a fundamental wholeness. The interplay of masculine and feminine can provide a powerful and creative thrust toward personal and spiritual growth. This can be illustrated by the following diagram. In the left portion the masculine and feminine aspects of one person are misunderstood to be conflicting opposites. Their interaction produces tension and confusion. However, as is shown in the right portion, if there will be only a slight re-orientation toward an ideal, the coming together of these two poles produces an impetus for growth toward that ideal.

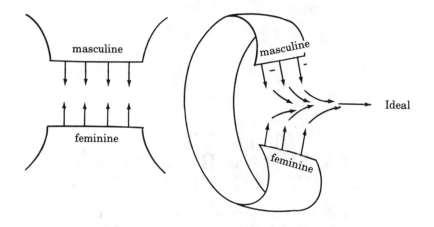

masculine

feminine

masculine

feminine

Ideal

Of course, for that creative impetus for growth to be properly directed there must be a balanced contribution from both poles. Otherwise, the arrows in the diagram will be misdirected.

We have now identified the three essential features for working creatively with what may have seemed to be opposites. The pair must be understood as aspects of One Force; each pole must be at least somewhat directed toward service to an ideal; and there must be a balanced contribution from the two. Although dreams can help us with all three of these features, they are especially involved in the third: encouraging us to a sense of balance between the polar aspects of living.

The concepts we have explored to this point are relevant to polarities other than masculine-feminine. They pertain as well to light-dark, process-form, wisdom-love, work-play, and many others. These concepts are particularly helpful in dealing with what appears to be a paradox.

A paradoxical situation is that in which it seems you just cannot win. Whenever you think you have it figured out you discover that the opposite can also be true. Some examples of rather abstract paradoxes are a Mobius strip (which seems to have only one side) and the nature of light (which seems to be both a wave and a particle). In daily life a common paradox is between mercy and punishment or between gentleness and discipline. When both poles can potentially create nearly equal benefits we may feel bewildered. When both poles seem nearly equal in truth we may feel confused. And yet it is in such situations that we must learn to operate. Our skill at handling paradoxical polarities to a large extent determines our growth. As Michael Murphy has written in his fascinating tale of sports and consciousness called *Golf in the Kingdom:* "The barometer of our spiritual enlightenment is how we deal with a paradox."

There are several ways of dealing with a paradoxical polarity. Frequently a person is paralyzed by it. Viewing the validity or value of both sides he may decide to do nothing. He just cannot bring himself to the apparent denial of one side which comes from adopting the other. A second way of dealing with a paradox is to act on one aspect of the polarity and deny the value or validity of the other. This leads to a rigid or dogmatic form of living in which balance and harmony are rarely achieved. Probably the superior method of dealing with a paradoxical polarity is to act on one aspect while simultaneously acknowledging the value of the other aspect. It is the application that is important, and it is usually not possible to apply both poles at the same time. The significant feature of this third approach is to retain a broad perspective that includes both poles while choosing to act on one of them.

Compensation and Balance

In previous chapters we have examined the principles of oneness and ideals. As was mentioned earlier in this chapter, there is a third feature in working creatively with a polarity. A balanced contribution from both poles keeps the movement for growth on target toward an ideal.

Carl Jung is the most notable dream theorist to point out the influence of dreams for balance. Briefly, his theory is that the relationship between the conscious and unconscious minds is compensatory in nature. For example, whenever we go to an extreme in our waking lives there is a need for balance. That extreme can be in thought, feeling or action. The response of the unconscious mind to such a situation is to produce the opposite extreme, so as to create a more balanced overall condition. The Jungian notion of compensation can be understood in ways other than just the balancing of extremes. However, this particular application of the principle proves to be very helpful in dream study.

Jung calls the psyche "a self-regulating system that maintains itself in equilibrium as the body does." Jung arrives at this conclusion after identifying what he calls a fundamental mistake in dream analysis: to assume that we can label the contents of the unconscious (e.g., the symbols and events of a dream) as unequivocally positive or negative. In other words, we cannot take a particular dream symbol and reliably say "that's a positive symbol" or "that's a negative symbol." We must interpret the dream *and* the dreamer. What may on the surface appear to be a "negative" content in a dream, may actually be an effort by the unconscious to compensate for conditions in waking life. For example, suppose one dreams of frivolous living. If he approaches the analysis with what Jung calls a naive view, he may assume that he can reliably call this dream content an unacceptable and negative attitude toward living. However, we must bring the waking life of the dreamer into the picture. If he has an extremely rigid and dour lifestyle, then the dream may have been doing a compensatory work—a balancing influence for these two poles of living.

Jung provides other illustrations of how a compensatory dream might work. In *Modern Man in Search of a Soul* he relates the dream of a young man. In the experience he watched his father driving away in a new car. He was doing a very clumsy job of driving and kept getting himself into a tight spot. Near the end of the dream he runs into a wall and wrecks the car. The dreamer shouts at him, telling him to behave himself. But the father only laughs and by his behavior reveals that he is quite drunk.

Despite a detailed consideration it seemed apparent that the dream did not apply to either the father or son's driving and drinking habits. Jung points out that this still left the question of why the unconscious of the young man felt compelled to produce "such an improbable story to discredit the father." He concluded that this was likely a compensatory dream which was needed to balance the son's attitude toward his father. Clearly the dream represents an extreme—one pole of a continuum of attitudes and feelings. It depicts the father as irresponsible and foolish. The other pole would be to idolize the father, to put him on a pedestal. What is needed is a balance between the two: respect and appreciation but also a sense of one's own value and importance. Jung says that this interpretative approach struck home with the dreamer.

As a final note, it is interesting to find that the notion of compensation and balance is not limited to Jung's definition of the dream process. In one Cayce reading we find a similar principle: "[Dreams] are those experiences that give the entity that mental balance for the full development of same." (900-257) In another passage we find a parallel phrase: "Oft [dreams] may be as opposite that which is presented to the body . . . " (1968-10)

Although Jung stresses this balancing of polar opposites through dreams more than does Cayce, the similarity suggests this is a significant tool to add to our repertoire of interpretative approaches.

As has been implied by the previous concepts and examples given in this chapter, there is a simple question whose answer can identify a compensatory dream. We ask ourselves, "Does this dream depict an extreme—of attitude, feeling or action?" If the answer is Yes, then follow with two other questions: "What is the opposite extreme?" And, "Am I living this opposite extreme in my daily life?" If the final answer is Yes then this is likely a dream of compensation, suggesting the need for greater balance between the two extreme poles. The actual interpretation of such a dream will be to express in daily life a greater degree of moderation.

In the example of the young man's dream, the first question is answered that the father is being depicted in an extremely unfavorable way. The opposite extreme would be to view him in an overly favorable way—to idolize him. The dreamer then sees that in fact that opposite extreme is being lived out in his conscious, waking life. And so, the applied interpretation of the dream would be to find a greater balance in outlook between these polar opposites.

Occasionally, the Cayce dream readings make use of this compensatory technique. The background for the following example is that the woman has abruptly decided that she should stop her habit of eating many sweets. As laudable as her change of heart may have been, it was too drastic a change for her body. Having become dependent on regular sugar intake, her body experienced this change as an extreme. To the consciousness of the body (and there is, in a sense, consciousness at the cellular level according to the readings) this extreme condition needed to be balanced. Toward this purpose a compensatory dream was produced.

Q-1. I was sitting at a table eating but more than eating—I was packing it in. There was chocolate cake and coconut cake and all kinds of sweets and goodies—and I just had a great time eating it all up.
A-1. In this there is presented to the entity, in this emblematical manner and way, the forces that are at work, as it were, in the physical being of the entity ... for as is seen, the entity recognizes in this the opposite from that being enacted in the daily life, see? ... Then eat more sweets, see? Not in excess, in moderation, for with all things let them be done in moderation, in decency and in order ...   136-21

The final line of this passage may seem unusual. However, we can assume that it is a gradual tapering off that is recommended. Even though the best diet may be no sweets, in this case she should begin with moderation and then decrease her intake.

This particular interpretative technique raises an important question. Are we looking for extremes in the subjective responses of the dreamer or in the events of a dream? For example, we see a dilemma in working with this dream.

> I am in a crowded stadium watching a football game. Suddenly I realize I am sitting there naked. Extremely embarraseed, I get up and try to get out of the crowd. However, I cannot find an exit.

In this case there are two types of extremes. First there is the extreme of having no covering and being totally exposed. Could this be the dream of a very shy, withdrawn person who never exposes any feelings or thoughts? On the other hand, the dream includes the subjective response by the dreamer of extreme embarrassment. Could this be the dream of a person who always wants to expose himself—emotionally or even physically? Either of these alternatives is conceivable and we should be prepared to look for dream compensation of both varieties. However, it is this writer's experience that the compensatory element is more often found in the *events* of the dream. That is, in the previous example, the probability is greater that the dreamer is very shy.

Further illustration of compensation from the Cayce dream readings may be helpful. In one instance (137-76, Q-4) a man related a dream interchange with colleagues at the Stock Exchange. Trouble was caused because he had unconsciously acted too light-heartedly with them. He ended up feeling badly for being too "smart aleckish." Cayce's commentary says that this dream "may be considered or treated as diagonal, or in the opposite of conditions." (137-76, A-4) The reading says that in waking life he is "too staid, or oldish in manner," a condition that is the opposite of the outgoing, "smark aleckish" behavior of the dream. Neither extreme is recommended; instead what is needed is an outgoing, friendly and warm manner in relationships at work.

We might also note that the subjective response of the dreamer—to feel badly about what he has done—is neither compensatory, nor is it an accurate assessment of the experience. If we depend on this emotional response, we miss the encouraging message of the dream toward greater light-heartedness. In effect the response of feeling badly about his behavior is a carryover from his conscious self-image of being staid. Even in the dream he misunderstands how valuable a more playful, open attitude toward relationships can be.

146

In a final illustration we see that those persons working with the theory of reincarnation may recognize another category of compensatory dreams. Apparently we may have past life recall dreams to balance us. In other words, if we have gone to an extreme it is possible to experience in dreams a previous lifetime which would tend to balance the present extreme. In the following instance a past life seems to have been quite a good one and is remembered in a dream during a period of extremes.

Q-2. *What was the significance of the two series of dreams I had a few years ago, in each of which I apparently lived another life?*
A-2. Study that as indicated and we will find that ye saw into those experiences especially with Naomi and Orpah and Ruth, and into those experiences in the hills of Judea.

These are the periods, as indicated, when the entity goes to the extreme. Keep that balance.   2175-1

Summary

The polarities of life can lead to creative growth rather than tension. However, for this to happen there are several requirements, all of which can be facilitated by dream study. We have already seen in previous chapters how dreams can teach us two of the required elements: a perspective of oneness and a recognition of ideals. In addition they can help us toward a more balanced contribution from each of the polar opposites. When this balanced condition exists, one is more likely to stay on track in growth toward an ideal.

This balancing can be achieved through a compensatory dream. By awakening the opposite of an extreme which is being lived in the waking state, the dream serves two purposes. First, it is doing an actual work of balancing. We might suppose that even if we do not recall or interpret a compensatory dream, it is still to some extent doing its job. And second, if we interpret the dream, it gives us applicable guidance to be expressing greater moderation and balance.

This chapter has also outlined a simple questioning process to identify these compensatory dreams.

Exercise in Application

Select a dream and make a list of the following items in the dream: (1) behaviors of self, (2) inner reactions of self, such as feelings, (3) behaviors of others on significant events, and (4) the theme of the dream. Then write down the opposite of each of these four types of items. If any of these items and their opposites seem to form a pair of polar extremes then ask yourself: "Am I living in my conscious, daily life the extreme opposite to the one in the dream?" If the answer is Yes, write out a course of action that would likely lead to greater balance between the two poles. Apply that course of action; and, if you are in a group, share your experience in application.

Chapter Twelve
DESIRE: THE BUILDING BLOCKS
OF DREAMS

Despite the fact that desires profoundly affect the course of our lives, they are not easy to define. We all experience desires, whether it be for things which are in keeping with our ideals or things which may sidetrack us in personal and spiritual growth. Perhaps what makes desire so difficult to define is that such a wide variety of things apparently fit this label, ranging from desires to know God to desires that may be self-destructive.

One clue to understanding desire which we find in the Cayce readings concerns the mental body. Just as the physical body is a collection of energy at the material level, the mental body can be understood as a collection of the mental patterns that have been built by an individual. Similarly, we might think of the spiritual body as a collection of the potentialities of the soul. Just as a person may exercise one muscle of the physical body so that it is stronger than the rest of the body, he might also magnify an aspect of the mental body or spiritual body so that it is especially pronounced.

However, our exploration of desire needs to specifically examine the nature of the *mental body*. The readings suggest that desire is particularly associated with this structure. Desire apparently is the activating influence that stimulates mental patterns. In the words of the readings, "For, as may be said, *desire* is that impluse which makes for the activity of the mental body . . . " (276-7) Of course, desire may be tied to a physical sensation (such as the desire for good-tasting food) and will likely have a manifestation in the physical body (such as gaining weight if one allows the desire for good-tasting food to predominate). Nevertheless it is at the level of the mental body where we must work with our desires and the patterns of mind which they habitually activate.

The work of attuning our desires to our ideals can be greatly facilitated through dream study and application. However, first it may be helpful to look at different types of desires. These are, of course, only broad categories of desire, yet they serve the purpose of aiding the self-analysis process.

A first type of desire might be called repeatability. In other words, we have had a particular experience before and we want to have it again. Most of our appetites are of this kind of desire. We must learn to distinguish a biological need from a desire if we are to develop beyond our present state of consciousness. For example, most of us eat frequently when there is no particular biological need (i.e., hunger) but there is a desire for something which tastes good. Usually a repeatability desire expresses itself as "I had that experience and I want it again." In our dreams it is often pointed out by situations in which we are fulfilling that desire or we are seeking gratification of that desire.

A second type of desire comes from a sense of incompleteness. It is a matter of wanting something we have missed out on. Usually we have a notion that if we were to have this experience which we have never had, then our lives would be happier in some way. Examples of this could be the desire to travel to a foreign country, or an unmarried person wanting to find a spouse. Like the first type of desire, we can find evidence of these patterns in our dreams (e.g., wish fulfillment dreams). To some extent desires of this second type may appear as compensatory dreams providing the experience of having something we have never had in waking life.

A third type of desire comes from the soul itself: the desire to know God. Just as there is a pattern of love among all the other patterns of our mind, so there is a desire to know God among all our other desires. As we have seen in a previous chapter, a dream of His Presence can reawaken this desire in our conscious lives.

Before looking more specifically at desire in our dreams, it may be useful to consider conscious efforts we can make to heal or uplift desires of the first two types. The problem with repeatability desires is that we have a mistaken concept of time, especially of the past and memory. What we need to do is realize that once we have had an experience it is written within our soul's memory, and it is always available to us from within. In this sense it is more appropriate to say to ourselves, "I *have* that experience" rather than "I had that experience and I must have it again right away." The difficulty we often encounter with repeatability desire is the frequency with which we feel compelled to reexperience what we already have. Although using the affirmation "I already have that experience within me" may not keep us from ever again following the desire pattern, it may serve to bring a better balance and more use of the will to decide when the desire will be followed.

In dealing with incompleteness-created desire, we should first redefine it in terms of inner things. We can ask ourselves, "If this desire were fulfilled how do I imagine I would feel differently?" Perhaps the answer is that we would feel happier or more worthwhile or more peaceful. In doing this we have re-identified what it is we really want—not necessarily the objective thing or event that may have been the focus of our desire, but rather an internal state of consciousness that is needed. When we have made this shift in perspectives, we may see alternative means of fulfilling that need. Often it can be done by giving to *another person* exactly what we have felt we need. For example, by giving love or encouragement to others we are likely to draw that experience to ourselves as well.

Identifying Desire in Dreams

When we examine the Cayce dream readings we discover that dreams can function to give a pictorial representation of the desires that most affect our lives. Since we are often so caught up in being who we are, it is likely that we do not recognize these directive influences. By giving them form, the dream state places them in a light where they can be identified and consciously measured against our ideals. This process of giving form quality to desires is an essential feature of dreaming.

There is a basic interpretative approach for discovering dreams which are not so much giving us direct guidance but are being produced as a reflection of our desire patterns. It involves simply asking oneself, "Does this dream merely depict something which I desire?" If the answer is Yes, then we must be careful in assigning any psychic quality to the dream. For example, suppose a man dreams that he wins the state lottery and upon analyzing the dream realizes that recently he has been thinking about how he would really like to be rich. In this case he should be careful not to make financial commitments based on the assumption that this extra money will soon be his. The dream may be only of a wish-fulfillment variety.

Nevertheless, there may be some precognitive quality to even this dream of riches. We can expect that this soul will have the opportunity to confront great wealth if he continues to strongly desire it. However, there is no promise of how soon that will happen or whether it will be very helpful to his spiritual growth when it comes. Here the perspective of reincarnation is needed. Our desire dreams of the present may be giving us a clue to what will happen in the distant future or even a future lifetime. When the desire finally manifests one may find that the soul is not able to use what comes in an especially growth-directed way. Therefore, when we use this interpretative technique and do find a desire depicted in the dream, then a second question is in order: "Is this desire in keeping with my ideals and if not how might I replace it?" The application in daily thoughts of the replacement desire can become the full interpretation of the dream.

Varieties of Dream Desires

Some of the desires we identify in our dreams will show us how they are *affecting our waking, physical lives* right now. A good example of this type concerns a man whose desire for fudge was creating a physical disturbance. Although he most likely had not linked his appetite for this food to his headaches, the dream reveals this current association.

Q-4. While asleep it seemed I tried to awaken but could not. As I fought to wake up the blood seemed to rush to my head and also gave me a headache. I then did wake up, thinking of making fudge.

A-4. . . . the subconscious force of the entity warning the entity as to the conditions of the physical forces, and that *through* which the condition becomes existent. That is, as is seen, the subconscious not able to wake—the change or flow of blood—headache, and with the headache, and the awakening desiring, physically, fudge. The mental forces are not subjugated sufficient as relating to desires (flesh) for the needs of the body. An over amount of those properties such as fudge *hinders* the circulation . . . 137-66

Another variety of desire dream shows how current desires could *affect future conditions*. What we have here is a matter of probability. Any desire has some sense of probability of being manifest physically. As we entertain the desire in imagination over and over, the probability increases. There comes a threshold point at which the probability becomes large enough so that our dreams begin to show future conditions if the desire continues to be followed.

What is that threshold point at which the dreams start coming? That probably depends on the desire and the overall purposes of the soul. For example, imagine that a soul comes into the earth with a strong sense of life purpose which depends on marrying a certain person. Apparently this was the circumstance in the life of Edgar Cayce himself, and it may be true for others as well. Also imagine that this hypothetical individual, in his early adulthood, begins to look at a woman with a desire for marriage. If it is not the right woman, we might expect that the probability threshold will be quite low. Because of a great sense of purposefulness within this soul regarding the marriage matter, it may be necessary to immediately depict in a dream what the consequences of the desire may lead to.

In another example, this one from the readings, the sexual attraction is a desire being depicted in the dream. The individual is warned in Cayce's interpretation that he will lose his spiritual insight in the future if he allows his sexual desires to overly control his life.

Q-5. My father appeared. Many were in our house. I was attracted to a woman by virtue of sex appeal. When I was a boy she had so attracted and appealed to me. I legitimized my relations to her by deserting my own wife and marrying her. I said, "Now it is all right. I am divorced and have married, so my relations are justified." My father denied that. I heard him in the bathroom, and when I wanted to get in, I couldn't. I carried on my relations. The scene changed. The moon was shining upon the earth. I saw its rays break through the clouds. Then my father or the voice spoke: "Redeemers are not meant to go about dreaming and romancing and idling under the moon. The next time you do this, I will take your sight away from you. You will lose your vision!"

A-5. ... these are of those conditions on which the entity has dwelt in mental forces ... that sex is as of the carnal mind, and of the earth earthy. Then, as applied in that way and manner as lessons, as given, there is seen that there is taken from any entity—this entity as well as others—that spiritual insight into the conditions as are of the spiritual nature, through indulgence in carnal conditions. Hence the rule, the lessons as have been given ... to be in the position of not an extremist in any nature or sense, for all force is of one force, but may be carried to the extreme to such an extent as to destroy the insight or the relations as one element of force to another. See?   900-268

A second dream shows the desire process in a more hopeful way. In this instance the dreamer is promised that if he continues to desire the conditions shown in the dream—and will work for it to happen—this can be interpreted as a precognitive dream. His desires and thoughts about it have already begun the building process that can result in the realization of a successful business in the future.

Q-6. Saw Ipsab Corporation as a huge and wealthy concern.
A-6. A presentation to the consciousness of conditions reasoned, weighed with subconscious and physical condition, for as the question had been turned over in the mind of the

entity, the subconscious builded that outcome which, if applied to the building up of such conditions, that *could* be the outcome of same. Then in applying same, use that condition in hand to begin, for the beginning must be made, would same grow into large conditions and prosperous ones. 137-50

A third variety of desire dream is what we might call *false ESP*. That is, even though the dream appears to be a psychic warning or a telepathic contact, it is actually a product of our desire to have such. For example, if a woman dreams that her employees are telling her that she is really doing quite a good job of supervising their work, is this dream a telepathic contact with those people? In this case we would want to analyze the dream and the dreamer. If she had been recently entertaining thoughts of what a good job she thought she was doing, then perhaps there is an implicit desire to have her employees say this, too. Her dream might only give a depiction of her desire for reinforcement, and not really be telepathic.

In a similar fashion, a dream from the readings can be interpreted as being desire-produced and false precognition. In this case the dreamer's husband apparently wanted her to go to Virginia Beach, and she did not especially want to make the trip. She recurrently dreamed (136-82) that there was an accident on the way to Virginia Beach. When they finally did make the trip they received a reading on the dream. Rather than an actual warning dream the reading described it as the product of her own thought processes, perhaps seeking an excuse for not having to make the trip. The reading also suggested that if she kept up this kind of mental process she would be building that event for future experiences.

As a final note on dreams of desire, we might wonder if these dreams should be *acted out*. Certainly, almost every dream should be *acted on* and there are *some* types of desire dreams that are best applied by directly carrying out the desire which is depicted. In one illustration, Edgar Cayce dreamed (294-82) that he talked with an acquaintance. The interpretation indicated that he had had a desire to speak with this individual and it was reflected in this experience. He is encouraged to act out the dream desire in daily life. Presumably it would involve no compromise of personal ideals to do so.

Fear in Our Dreams

Like desire, fear can be a building block of our dream experiences. In fact, one way of looking at fear is to see it as a type of desire. This may sound strange because hardly anyone wants to be afraid. But we must look deeper at fear and see that at its root there is a type of desire: to hold on to present conditions. Those conditions may be exterior or they may be the conditions of our self-concept. As an example of the second instance, the fear of death might be viewed as the desire to hang on to the notion of oneself as a physical body.

From this perspective fear often becomes a desire of the first type: the desire for repeatability. It is the emotional response we may have when threatened that a self-image or an exterior situation may no longer be repeatable.

It is no wonder that fear is the most paralyzing of emotions in our spiritual growth! It is rooted in the desire to hang on to things as they are—to keep from changing or growing. Even the fear created by a trauma in the past fits this view of the process. Having achieved some degree of stability since the painful occurrence, we may fearfully hold on to the new circumstances. The fact that past experience has taught us how vulnerable our stability is, we are all the more likely to desire what we have now. Unfortunately, our adaptation to life since the painful episode may be only a coping mechanism. If we insist on keeping the coping mechanism we are likely to block a true healing. For example, imagine a teenager who was beaten by his father as a child. Now he is afraid of men and withdraws. He is fearful whenever he is left alone with a man. The withdrawal from male figures is a coping device which will never heal the problem. And yet we can sympathize with his desire to hold on to the adaptive stability he has achieved.

Interpreting the Dream as Fear

We are encouraged in the readings to pay special attention to dreams that involve fear. They may indicate either significant warning dreams or special indicators of what is blocking our growth. One reading says that dreams are "experiences in emblematical ways and manners that are to be heeded or taken note of. Especially do we find this true when such impressions are gathered in the body consciousness as to bring that of fear... " (538-35)

The basic question we ask ourselves in order to interpret a dream which may have been produced by fear is this: Does this dream bring me an experience which I consciously fear? It may well be that fear is not the emotion awakened in the dream itself, and yet the cause of the dream is a conscious or unconscious fear. It is probably wise to ask ourselves this question in analyzing any dream which has a troublesome outcome. It will be difficult to determine if it is actually a warning dream, until we can answer, "No, I do not consciously fear what my dream depicts."

Consider a series of experiences from a man and woman whose dreams we have already examined extensively. At one time she reports, "Dreamed that I could never have a child—that none would ever come to me—that I would never give birth." (136-16, Q-3) If fear is a type of desire, we might ask, "What is the desire in this case?" It is the desire to keep a realistic hope of becoming a mother. The dream seems to undermine this and fear is the emotional response. Most likely the dream is a replay of a conscious fear she has every time she doubts that she can ever become pregnant. Cayce's commentary indicates that the dream is merely the product of a conscious fear she holds in mind.

Q-3. Dreamed that I could never have a child—that none would ever come to me—that I would never give birth.
A-3. This again is a mental condition that is being carried through the entity's forces, and presents only that of the mental . . . Hence the lesson that is necessary for the preparations for such a condition—motherhood, the highest service to the Maker . . . This will occur. Child will be born. Necessary that these [preparations] be carried out, however, as pertaining to the law concerning such . . .   136-16

In another dream she is apparently now pregnant and her husband is fearful. He dreams: "Saw [my wife] start to spot or menstruate—the first sign of a miscarriage. She was surprised and startled. Both of us were disappointed." (900-269) In the analysis of this dream there is indicated a fear-based origin.

. . . has been some fear, some doubt, as to the full complete understanding. Then, put self in that attitude as is necessary to bring that force as gives the building of all creative energy in the right way and manner. Not an indication that this would happen. Rather the indication of the fear within the entity itself that it would happen, see? . . .   900-269

In a third example of this couple, the wife reported: "Dreamed my husband . . . wasn't coming home any more and I cried bitterly." (136-9, Q-1) Is this predictive of a marriage break-up or at least of a deteriorating relationship? Quite to the contrary, in this case the dream meant that the marriage was growing stronger! As the love between the two was deepening, the wife began to have fears (perhaps unconscious) that they might become separated. For her, greater closeness meant more vulnerability to separateness and loneliness. This fear is depicted in the events created by the dream.

If she had not had Cayce to interpret the dream she might have asked, "Does this dream give me an experience of something which I fear?" With a little self-analysis she would have seen this was the case. Her next step would have required her to replace that fear (through prayer, meditation, counseling, discussion with her husband, etc.) with trust and faith. If the dream continued to reoccur she might be more likely to assume that the dream is warning of an impending marriage trouble.

In a final example from this couple, the husband dreamed: "[An acquaintance] criticizing me since I had but two years of college, therefore denying any claim I had to knowledge. What degree or diploma had I to show that entitled me to any position based upon academic or scientific knowledge?" (900-331, Q-1) We might wonder if this dream is a realization that he needs more formal education. If we assume, as some dream interpreters do, that the dreamer's understanding *in the dream* is most reliable, then we are led to this conclusion. However, Cayce's analysis was not this at all. His approach suggested that the dreamer merely was fearful that he was not educationally adequate and could have been exposed or criticized for his lack of formal schooling.

Fear Awakened in Dreams

In contrast to a dream *produced* by fear, there are others which directly stimulate fear. We should pay particular attention to these experiences, not because the dreamer's fearful reaction is always appropriate, but because frequently the readings indicate that the fear correctly identifies a warning. In one case a woman dreamed that she should not have another child, and that if she did insanity would follow. (140-30) In the commentary by the reading the emotion of fear was identified as the one awakened in the dream. It is suggested that this is a warning dream—that, in fact, she should get her attitudes and physical condition in order before becoming pregnant. Fear need not be the appropriate response to the problem, but it did identify the dream as one worth studying carefully. Here the re-dreaming technique may work best. Having defined the dream as a possible warning, she could relive the dream in reverie and replace her response to the words that were told her. The warning is still the same but replacing fear with hope and commitment is the first step toward making the needed life style changes.

Summary

What we see in the events of our dreams are largely our own thought forms. That is, our mental activities in daily life create

157

the images that will be used in our dream life. Desires—as the *activating* influence of our mental patterns—can therefore be seen as a major contribution to the dream-creation process. They can constitute the building blocks of our dream experience.

The Freudian notion of wish fulfillment dreams is viewed as naive by some people who claim to have discovered transpersonal or spiritual dimensions of dreaming. However, the Cayce readings indicate that *some* dreams are just that—a depiction of what we have consciously or unconsciously wanted to happen. Admittedly the strong desire may eventually lead to the desired conditions in the physical world. However, this may take a long period of time. We are interested in discovering how the dreamer can *immediately* apply the dream; and in the case of a desire-created experience, that application often involves examining and transforming the desire.

Three types of desire have been outlined: repeatability, incompleteness and God-directed. The concepts of this chapter have focused on the first two of these. In addition, dreams involving fear may be seen as a subset of repeatability desires. A relatively simple questioning process can get us started toward identifying dreams of desire or fear.

Exercise in Application

Select a dream that does not overtly involve the emotions of fear or desire on your part as the dreamer. Ask yourself, "Does this dream merely depict something which I desire?" If so, try to identify it as one of three types: repeatability, incompleteness or God-directed. Then determine a way of applying this insight. If it is a repeatability desire try using the suggested affirmation in daily life. If it is incompleteness try the steps described earlier which involve translating it into internal rather than external things. If it is God-directed, decide on a procedure which may reflect that desire in waking life (e.g., a more regular meditation period).

If the dream does not show evidence of desire, consider that it may be fear-produced. Ask yourself, "Does this dream bring me an experience which I consciously fear?" If the answer is Yes then do not jump to the conclusion that this is a precognitive dream. Instead decide on a replacement attitude or emotion for the fear and work on holding that replacement in mind. Observe any changes which may occur in your dream life.

If neither of these approaches seems to work on the first dream you select, then use another dream. If you are in a group which works with dreams, share your experiences in applying this process on one dream.

Chapter Thirteen
DESTINY OF THE BODY: PHYSICAL ATTUNEMENT THROUGH DREAMS

Contained within the microcosm of the human body is the macrocosm of the univese. Within the cells of our physical bodies and their inter-related functions we find a model of all that takes place in creation. This, in itself, points to the significance of our physical selves. The pattern of any experience or condition we seek can be found within us.

In addition to this principle of the macrocosm in the microcosm, there is a further special significance of the human body. It permits us as souls to have a unique kind of experience. The physical body allows us to partake of materiality in such a way that we can master this dimension of experience.

How does it permit us to do this? First, by providing a vehicle for the *focusing of consciousness.* In other words, by occupying a physical form, the mind and soul must be specific—they must operate in the confines of time and space. Those confines can be a blessing, however. They allow our souls to discover the laws of loving in small increments such as a single human life. Without a physical body and accompanying conscious mind, many souls would find development quite difficult.

There is a second perspective on how the human body allows us to experience a mastery of this dimension. It concerns the very way in which the physical body is constructed. The Cayce readings and many other teachings suggest that there are sensitive centers within the body which relate to the development of higher states of consciousness. These spiritual centers or *chakras* (to use the ancient Sanskrit term) are seven in number. They represent seven broad categories of consciousness and are a physical representation in the human body of the connection between our human selves and divine selves. (For a more detailed discussion of these centers see *Meditation and the Mind of Man.)*

The importance of the physical body is particularly underscored if we consider the purpose for our being here in the earth. Is it to learn to cope with difficulties? Is it to discover a way to transcend our attachments to earthly life? These possible answers and dozens of others have been offered. And yet there is one answer that seems to best reflect the spirit of the teachings in the Bible as well as the Cayce readings: to express in our lives as individuals the love of God. In other words, to bring the infinite *into* finite expression. Clearly the physical body must play an important role if this is to take place. The body should not be seen as an obstacle which binds us to materiality. In fact the desires that we attribute to the body are usually more a part of the mind. Rather we should see the physical body as the very vehicle through which we can fulfill our destiny—the infinite in the finite.

It should be of little wonder to us that nearly two-thirds of the readings given by Edgar Cayce concerned people's physical problems. It would be naive to assume that this happened simply because two-thirds of the requests were for physical readings. Rather, a part of the reason lies in the insight that many people will not start looking for answers until they start hurting. And as a type of "answer-giver" the psychic Cayce attracted many hurting people. The same held true in the life of Jesus.

However, more importantly we must see in the life of Jesus and Edgar Cayce a profound awareness that the body is significant. It hinders God's plans and purposes for mankind when the physical form is less than whole. The infinite coming into the finite will manifest as healing—even physical healing. We can expect that it was for this reason—to help the infinite more effectively come into the finite—that the major portion of Edgar Cayce's psychic work was in giving physical readings.

And so, we might ask, what does this have to do with dreams? Is not the dream experience the one remaining contact that each soul has frequently with *non-material* life? And yet simply because the dream experience is closely tied to our growth in awareness it often teaches us about the body. Because a balanced, healthy body can be a great asset to growth in consciousness, dreams will often concern themselves with our physical condition.

It is, of course, nothing new to say that dreams are related to the body. There have been periods of history when many people thought that all dreams were produced by conditions in the physical make-up. For example, some have supposed that the dream image of a muddy street would have been produced by existing conditions in the intestines of the dreamer. A water pump might have represented the function of the heart. In other words, this perspective suggested that dreams were merely pictorial representations of what was going on at that moment in the sleeping body.

Although there is now strong evidence to reject that all dreams are produced in this way, further research has uncovered other relationships between the physical body and dreaming. There appear to be distinct physiological correlates of dreams. That is, when particular conditions happen in a sleeping body, it is highly likely that a dream is taking place. This is known as REM (Rapid Eye Movement) sleep, and it is characterized by more than just the quick eye shifts from which it derives its name. There is a recognizable brain wave pattern. Using an electroencephalograph a researcher can recognize when a REM period is probably taking place. During REM periods there are also changes in the tone of the muscles, in the resistivity of the skin to an electrical current, and in males a penile erection. For a more detailed discussion of the physiological correlates of dreaming, the reader is encouraged to study Robert Van de Castle's *On The Psychology of Dreaming.*

However, merely recognizing that the body goes through distinct changes when a dream takes place does not mean the dream is *about* the physical body. Nearly every dream theorist will admit that there are specific bodily conditions associated with the process of dreaming; however, many theorists are reluctant to link the *meaning* of dreams to physical conditions. There is a strong tendency to associate the meaning of dreams to psychological conditions. From such a point of view, a dream about the physical body would concern only the attitudes or emotions the dreamer had about his or her own body (e.g., ashamed of it, afraid it will get sick, proud of the way its beauty gets attention from others).

It is at just this point that the Cayce readings make a major contribution to the literature of dream theories. They suggest that a major role of the dream experience is to provide information to the conscious mind about conditions of the physical body. We have seen that Edgar Cayce's psychic work laid strong emphasis upon healing the body as a part of fulfilling the soul's destiny in the earth. Similarly the Cayce dream readings put a strong emphasis on the feedback and guidance our dreams give us in our efforts to achieve psychical attunement.

Types of Physical Dreams

There are at least three categories of dream experience that we should look for in recognizing a physical dream. In working with these categories, however, we should not become too rigid. In other words, when we see that a particular dream fits a given category of physical dream, we should keep in mind that it may *also* fit other categories as well. And we should also keep in mind that a dream which seems to be primarily psychological in nature may also have elements that give us clues about physical conditions. As we develop this capactiy to work simultaneously with a dream at several levels of interpretation, we uncover the richness of meaning found in almost every dream. Briefly, three categories of physical dreams are as follows:

Physically produced dreams. Such experiences can be the result of external or internal conditions. Most of us have had an experience something like this: one dreams of being in Arctic regions during a blizzard, only to awaken and find that the window was left open and a cold draft was blowing across the bed. In other words, we may occasionally have dreams that are largely produced by the sleeping conditions in which we have placed the body: the temperature of the room, noise coming into the room, etc.

Perhaps more importantly, there are physically produced dreams that are derived from internal conditions. In Cayce's readings this was especially true of the influences of diet and the digestive system. Nevertheless, *any* physiological condition apparently has the potential to produce a dream. What seems to be the common factor within this category of dream experience (no matter what bodily system is involved) is a tendency for such dreams to be confusing or troublesome. An example of this is found in the following question and answer exchange.

Q-11. *what is causing me mental unrest and as a result disturbing dreams?*

A-11. This unbalanced condition—not wholly coordination between the superficial circulation, or the circulation that is the more active in the sensory forces, and the deeper circulation to the organs of the body. Thus the activity of the mind, or the sympathetic and cerebrospinal force of mind, causes dreams, see?   2772-4

In other passages it is the digestive system that is linked to nightmares. Stress or upset in that system is bound to cause an effect upon the subconscious mind, which controls its activity. The result can be a bizarre dream that seems tangled and pointless. Apparently it was this kind of confused, senseless dream experience that Edgar Cayce referred to as a "nightmare," rather than the elaborate dream story at the end of which we awaken frightened. This frightening dream may likely have a *psychological* origin. But Cayce's nightmare terminology—defined as "without any specific heads, tails or points" (294-40)—refers to a dream caused by digestive imbalances.

To make these principles applicable we can turn them into questions. Does my dream show evidence of merely incorporating my external sleeping conditions? If so, we may need to look no deeper for a meaning. Does my dream seem unusually bizarre and pointless, without a "specific head or tail"? If so, then we should recall what we ate the night before. If our diet shows evidence of potential digestive upset, the dream may be only a product of these conditions.

As a final note on dreams of this category, it is interesting to recognize a hypothesis in the readings about physically produced dreams. Again, it concerns the digestive system and the quality of our dream experiences. It suggests that if we will experiment with a vegetarian diet we will see a change in our dreams.

> ... the same body fed upon *meats,* and for a period—then the same body fed upon only herbs and fruits—would *not* have the same character or activity of the other self in its relationship to that as would be experienced by the other self in its activity through that called the dream self.   5754-1

You may wish to experiment with this hypothesis and see what results you find for such physically produced dreams.

Physical warning dreams. In the first category there were dreams produced by conditions that already exist in the body. However, dreams can also provide us with a warning about conditions likely to come in the body, even though they may not as yet be manifested in the flesh. Obviously it is to our benefit to begin to recognize and act upon these physical warning dreams.

There are numerous examples of this in the Cayce dream readings. One man dreamed that while riding on a train he struck up a conversation with an older man sitting opposite him. The older man said, "Such a long trip is tiresome—one's legs ache right here (indicating above the knees) from sitting so long." The dreamer agreed that it was tiresome and felt how his own legs hurt. Cayce's interpretation was very straightforward. This was a warning that unless the dreamer started getting more exercise, he would soon have those very leg problems. (900-167)

In another instance the same man dreamed that he was expectorating blood into his handkerchief. He was very frightened in the dream, fearing tuberculosis. As the dream closes he is frantically trying to reach Cayce for a reading to determine the cause of the blood. In waking life, he received a reading on this dream and was told that it was a warning dream about his body. These exact conditions could become a physical reality if he allowed himself to continue under the same kind of strain in daily living. (900-262)

Of course, not all physical warning dreams will be as explicit as these two examples. In the following instance the physical warning dream is presented in a more symbolic way.

Q-8. I was in Newark as it was years ago when we used to live there, and was riding on a trolley car up close to Clinton Avenue, and lost my raincoat. The trolley car ran over it.

A-8. In this we find that relating to the health of the individual, in an emblematical manner, that entity should use same, then, as a warning, keeping body dry, keeping feet dry, else the cold, the congestion, as comes from same, would prove the detrimental manner as is seen in dream—the loss of garments appears to the entity, see? 137-24

Without having a psychic interpret this dream, how might the dreamer have recognized this as a warning dream? One way would have been to work with a theme for the dream: I lose something which protects my body and health from the weather. The dreamer might then have seen that this theme was applicable to the way he was treating his body in daily life—not protecting himself from conditions that might lead to a cold.

Health problems solved. In the initial chapter of this book, dreams were defined in terms of six functions they perform, one of which was to solve problems. Such problems are not only mental and emotional, but physical as well. The solution can even come when we do not yet realize there is a problem!

The solution to a physical problem is found in the following dream. A woman dreamed, "It was raining starch and I dreamed that I should go out in the rain of starch and put it on my side to ease the pain." (136-49) Cayce commented that this was the solution to her recent physical ailments: she needed more starch in her diet. In this case there was a sort of play on the word "starch." We should be especially alert for such puns in looking for solution dreams.

Occasionally, the solution will be presented in a very direct manner, even though it involves something that had never been consciously considered. One young man had had chronic skin eruptions on his back. He dreamed that a middle-aged woman came up to him in the course of a rather lengthy dream and merely said, "You ought to put rubbing alcohol on your back each day." When he applied this treatment it brought a large measure of healing. One thing was interesting about this dream and many others which give us information about the physical body. The bulk of the dream seemed to be about certain psychological and emotional issues in his life. Although it is conceivable that those issues could have been the very ones creating the physical disturbance, in some cases this does not seem to be true. We need to be alert for insertions in our dreams which give us physical body guidance, even though most of the dream is about something else.

How to Recognize Physical Dreams

Our challenge is to identify these potentially valuable sources of information about physical attunement. Our destiny is to express the infinite in the finite and to a large degree that requires a body which is as attuned and healed as possible. So we can expect that our dreams will occasionally—or even frequently—be giving us this type of help. We can identify physical dreams by the following approaches.

The setting. It is probably our tendency with most any dream to fail to take enough notice of the setting. It can be an extremely worthwhile exercise for recognizing a physical dream. Although it is far from a foolproof technique, a consideration of the setting is often the easiest way to discover a physical dream. When the setting is the kitchen or dining room there is a good chance it is a dream about diet. When the setting is the bathroom, it is likely a dream about physical cleansing or eliminations. If the setting is a doctor's office or hospital, it may not be immediately clear what body function is involved, but there is a likelihood that the dream concerns physical health needs.

In one example the setting of a drugstore provided a good interpretative clue. A man dreamed that he went into a New York City drugstore. A woman doctor treated him for his sore toe. The salve she rubbed on his toe was made from tortoise shell. He noticed while he was in the store that other people were eating ice cream and sodas. Cayce interpeted this as a physical dream concerning the digestive system and the blood supply related to the digestion. He said, "The woman representing then as a lesson, or as a guide, that the entity should *not* partake of too much sweets that become as tortoise shell to the digestion, especially to the blood supply." (900-228) In other words, the high intake of sweets was slowing down the blood supply and hindering the digestive process.

The setting of the neighborhood of a drugstore provides a clue in another experience of the same dreamer. In the dream, he and his brother were on their way to visit some relatives but wanted to stop at a certain drugstore on the way. It was night and they got lost. They were frightened away from one street by an ugly-looking individual. Then they came to a gathering of many people, and while his brother talked with a crippled person, the dreamer sought out his bearings and the store. There were many tough, threatening people about. Finally, he saw the store, but the way to it was blocked by an ugly individual. (900-322, Q-3) Cayce's interpretation suggested that this is a physical warning dream—that in waking life the dreamer needed to be careful of the way in which he used drugs for certain ailments.

Body part depicted. Whenever a particular part of the body has a role in the dream we can anticipate that this may be a physical dream. Again, it is not a foolproof technique but a good rule of thumb for quickly recognizing dream guidance for physical attunement.

In one instance a woman dreamed that she dove into water from a rickety platform which seemed very unsubstantial in structure. In diving in she made a belly whopper—i.e., she landed on her stomach, and it hurt. (136-22, Q-1) In this case the stomach or belly region played a key role in the dream. In fact Cayce interpreted this as a physical dream: that her body was not prepared for the pregnancy she hoped for. Two months later she had a miscarriage.

In another example, a particular body part is especially prominent in the dream and yet it does not literally depict the primary problem area. Edgar Cayce dreamed that he was crazy and was looking into his head. He fixed a wheel in his head that had stopped running due to a particle of dirt getting into it. (294-56, Q-1) The reading on the dream suggested that this was a physical dream (as we might have guessed because of the significant role played by the head in the dream events). However, the primary problem was in the *digestive system.* Poor eliminations were leading to pressure on the nerves and a resulting influence on the brain. The physical repair work needed was much like that done in the dream: to oil or lubricate the system so that the drosses might be removed.

A final consideration about body parts is that a pun or play on words may be used. In the previous dream about the sweets and the tortoise shell, the reader may have wondered why the big toe played such an important role. Cayce's interpretation of this was that it merely represented the slang expression "sore toe," to mean an especially troublesome condition.

Thematic approach. A final technique for recognizing a physical dream is to find where the theme of the dream fits a physical condition. This has already been suggested in the dream of the lost raincoat. It would work as well in Cayce's own dream of fixing the wheel in his head. A theme might be: foreign material stops things from running properly. He might have then seen that the theme was applicable to the recent condition of his eliminative system. The applicability of the thematic approach is demonstrated in the following example.

Q-1. I was at what seemed to be a family party. We were eating refreshments when Edward Blum and someone started to fight. Hot words led to a fist fight and I finally separated them.   900-234

At first glance this may appear to be a message about the dreamer's emotional make-up (perhaps suppressed hostility) or even a psychic dream about Edward Blum. However, the setting is a party where people are eating and should at least alert us to the possibility of a physical dream. Furthermore, we see that one theme of the dream is: I must intervene in the conflict between two parties. In the dreamer's life that theme of conflict was very applicable to what happened in his body when he overindulged in sweets. The reading states:

A-1. In this there is presented to the entity that warning as to the diets in the physical forces of the body; for, as has been given that the entity should be warned as respecting that that is taken in the system, especially in the way of sweets and of those things that overload the weakened condition in the red blood supply of the body.   900-234

The thematic approach is a very versatile one and can often help us identify those physical dreams which do not include the clues of setting or body part.

Summary

The destiny of the physical body is to be the vehicle for expression of the infinite. Rather than being an obstacle to spiritual growth, as some have supposed, the body can be viewed as a great asset. Nevertheless, it is only as the body is brought into attunement with the mind and spirit that it can fulfill this destiny.

Dreams provide frequent feedback to the conscious mind so that greater physical health can be achieved. This especially takes place through warning dreams (alerting the dreamer to unforeseen physical problems) and solution dreams (in which a diagnosis and/or treatment procedure is suggested).

Although many physical dreams will be immediately obvious, others will be clothed in symbolic terms and are more difficult to identify. Both the setting of the dream and the appearance of specific body parts in the dream events can be effective interpretative clues. The very versatile theme approach can also be helpful in recognizing a dream related to the physical body.

Exercises in Application

Consider the types of possible dream setting which for you might be indicators of physical dreams. Make a list of those settings, and next to each one write the aspect of your physical body to which it is likely to relate (e.g., kitchen—diet; health spa—exercise). Compare your list with others in your group.

Then take a series of dreams (perhaps one week's worth) and select those dreams which include any of the settings on your list. Identify places in these dreams in which a particular body part plays an important role. Use the theme method on any dream that does not include a significant role for a body part. Using this approach decide which of the dreams seem to be giving you feedback on your physical condition. Are there any recurrent messages?

Now try to discover and then apply an *application* of each physical dream you have identified. Get some help from other members of your group in deciding on specific things to do in applying these physical dreams.

Chapter Fourteen
SPIRIT: THE CERTAINTY OF SURVIVAL

There are common denominators that link all mankind: the indwelling spirit and the gift of free will are two examples. Another is physical death. Every person can anticipate the experience of this transition. And death is just that—a transition from one dimension of living to another dimension of living.

Are we prepared to die? Do we know anything concering what may be in store for us on the other side of the veil which separates material from non-material life? We may be reassured that the answer is yes. Through the process of sleeping and dreaming we rehearse dying each night.

Just as the rehearsal of a theater production is not identical to the circumstances of the opening night performance, there is still enough similarity that valuable training can take place. In the same way there may be certain qualitative differences between dreams and the after-death experience. However, the process of sleeping and dreaming is so similar to dying that we can learn much from dreams about life on the other side.

In discussing the nature of the sleep state, the Cayce readings call it "a shadow of, that intermission in the earth's experience of, that state called death . . . " (5754-1) Just as the shadow cast by an object is not precisely the object itself, it does give us important clues about the object's appearance. Sleeping and dreaming give us a nightly introduction into the realm of non-material life.

The Quality of the After-Death Experience

Recently several researchers have reported case studies of persons who were revived after having been pronounced dead in hospitals. Hundreds of these cases exist, frequently involving several minutes in which the patient is apparently dead and yet is subsequently resuscitated by doctors. Until recently most such patients kept quiet about remarkable experiences they may have had in the interim period—perhaps fearing they would not be taken seriously.

Dr. Raymond Moody, for one, has made a systematic effort to identify and interview these people and has reported his findings in the best-selling book *Life After Life*. Despite the fact that most if not all individuals interviewed had never met each other, there were remarkable parallels in their experiences. Nearly every one of these common dimensions of near-death experience are anticipated by concepts in the Cayce readings.

One of the most significant of the common experiences is that of reviewing the entirety of one's life. Every minute detail of the individual's life is viewed simultaneously, often in a panoramic display. The parallel principle from the readings is that at death the subconscious mind (i.e., the storehouse of memories of all our past experiences) becomes the conscious mind.

We might well ask, "If sleeping and dreaming are shadows of dying, then do our dreams make us conscious of the subconscious mind?" The answer is a qualified yes. The dream experience is rarely as dramatic as the near-death experience in which there is a panoramic view of everything one has done. However, in our dreams there is a measure of becoming aware of things that have been stored within the subconscious. A frequent example of this process is dreaming of a person one has not even thought of for years.

The important thing to remember about dreams in this regard is that they serve to remind us. They show us that nothing is forgotten in the mind of the soul. We will, at the appropriate time, once again become conscious of events and people that have been pushed off into the subconscious mind and out of conscious consideration. On the one hand the prospect of such remembering may not seem very attractive (there are things we would all just as soon forget forever!). Yet from another perspective we see that this is a blessing to us. The experiences and events of the past continue to influence us, even though they may be forgotten. Often such influences bring pain, confusion or self-doubt. And so the prospect of making them conscious once again includes the potential of healing them. It can happen little by little through our dreams and apparently it can happen in our initial experiences after death.

What else can we anticipate about the after death experience? Again there are many clues from the dream readings. We are drawn to experience with like-minded souls. That is, there are many planes or dimensions of consciousness, and as souls we are drawn in awareness to that one which best serves our needs for growth. We are likely to encounter other souls and have experiences with them as we do here in materiality.

Unfortunately, for the person who has committed suicide, it is likely that his or her experiences are quite troublesome. We can never escape from ourselves and the place in consciousness after suicide is likely to be even more painful than the one preceding.

Do we have a body in the after-death state? That is not an easy question to answer if for no other reason than that we have a limited notion of body. In the sense of a flesh body with appetites such as sex and hunger, the answer is probably no. However, for some of the dimensions of after-death experience there may be a body in the sense of a vehicle through which to focus consciousness. Such a body might be called a finer physical body, an astral body or an etheric body. The point is that any such body is created by the soul (just as the flesh body is) because it provides a vehicle for the experiences one needs.

It may well be that in the initial periods after death we appear to ourselves to have bodies because we believe we require a body to experience. Although we are actually infinite, pure consciousness, we do not fully realize that yet. As we move on and grow in awareness after death we may reach dimensions in which a body as we know it is no longer needed. It is interesting to note, however, that in the dreams of most people, the dreamer has a body through which he or she experiences in the dream. This can be likened to our belief that we require a body of some sort in the after-death state.

As a final note about the quality of life after death, we might consider an uninterpreted dream of Edgar Cayce about the borderland (i.e., that dimension of experience just after death). This unique dream is published in the Library Series of Edgar Cayce readings entitled *Dreams and Dreaming,* Part I, pages 435-438. In the dream Cayce found himself in the borderland with his wife and secretary. They decided that they should carry on the work of helping others just as they had in the earth. They enlisted the aid of a man they knew from earthly life and he helped them construct the proper building. At one point the man asked Cayce, "But tell me, have you seen any of these people we expected to see in heaven? Because this is heaven, ain't it?" Cayce answered that he was not sure but he felt they were on the right road!

Then they began to have meetings in their new building. People came who needed help. Apparently many did not realize that in this after-death state there was work that needed to be done. Since there was no longer the harshness of material life, many souls had decided that all they had to do was just sit around, making no efforts to grow in awareness or serve others. Many had also forgotten who they were. In this dream Cayce began to give readings for people. His work was to help "find out for people *who they were, and what they wanted to do!*" This dream seems to particularly point out that it is necessary to keep an attitude after death of seeking to know ourselves more fully and of being of greater service to others.

Communication in Dreams with the Departed

When we dream of a person who has died there are several ways to work with interpreting such an experience. The dream character of the departed one may represent a part of oneself. This is probably most likely the case when we dream of a deceased individual whom we did not know personally. For example if you dream of Abe Lincoln it is most likely that he symbolizes a particular quality in yourself.

Another interpretative approach to consider—especially when the dead person is a close relative—is that the dream has happened to help you confront your feelings about the person and his or her death. For example, such a dream may be a confrontation with one's sadness or even resentment at the parting. The image of the person may appear in the dream because it stimulates this needed meeting between one's feelings (perhaps repressed) and conscious awareness.

However, a third possibility is that this is a genuine contact or communication with the deceased person. The dreamer's mind, while in the sleep state, is more closely attuned with the mental state of the deceased than it would normally be in the waking hours. There are many instances in the Cayce dream readings in which a valid communication has been made in this way.

Apparently the two most influential factors in permitting this kind of contact are attunement and love. The principle found in several of Cayce's dream interpretations can be stated as follows: When the superconscious mind rules (i.e., provides the directive influence) contact is possible between the subconscious minds of a dreamer and a person who has died. Such an influence from the superconscious is particularly enhanced through attunement procedures such as meditation. This notion is found in the following passage, along with a warning that it may not be helpful to the other soul to press for such contact too often. It may be that such efforts on the part of those still living in materiality bind the departed soul and keep it from moving on to higher dimensions of experience.

Q-1. How may this body attune his mind with that of his father who has gone from this earth's sphere?
A-1. Just as has been given. Study into the borderland, as has been given; with the study, the thought, the lapsing of the self

into these conditions, where the consciousness is laid aside and the superconscious rules, we may come into such communications, as this body has in sleep. Not well that this be dwelt upon at all times, for we bring to the other entity distresses at times.   900-8

The second influential factor in such communication is love. Dr. Harmon Bro, a minister and psychotherapist, has found in studying the Cayce dream readings (some of which he observed firsthand) that love is the key element in dream contact with the dead. When the departed one apparently comes in a dream to give information (e.g., what to do in the stock market) we must be very careful about acting literally on it. However, when the dream of the departed one seems to bring assurances that love and life continue beyond the grave, then we can with greater assurance assume that this has been a genuine communication.

Looking more closely at the types of genuine communication we may experience, there are at least four varieties.

To comfort the dreamer. Loved ones who have passed on are frequently concerned for our understanding of what has happened. From the perspective of a soul in the borderland the continuity of life may be more clear than to a soul still in materiality. Through a dream communication the dreamer can receive the gift of assurance and comfort. This is indicated in the following two examples.

Q-2. I was not thinking of J.S. who died three weeks before Mother—how and why did this entity transmit the message to me?
A-2. . . . there may be seen how that friendship, the love of one close, near and dear, is ready to give that aid, when one attunes self . . . For, as is seen then in this presented, that the entity may know, *not alone* does the mother go out; not alone in that unseen world, yet with that same care, that same love, raised to a better understanding of the forces as are manifested.   136-33

Q-11. What is the significance of my continual dreaming of my husband [deceased]?
A-11. Just as has been outlined. Will the body—*not* unbalancing self in mind or way, but heed those conditions that are presented, they *still* may assist, guide, help and *comfort* the body, in the material, the physical, and the spiritual plane, and they seek to do such.   2218-1

To guide the dreamer. Although we must be careful to measure any such potential guidance by our ideals, there may be instances in which a recommended course of action by the deceased person should be heeded. Particularly in matters of health and service we should pay careful attention to seeming communication with a departed loved one. This is well illustrated in the following question and answer exchange.

Q-4. My mother appeared to me. I saw her very distinctly. She said to me: "You should go to the osteopath. You ought to be ashamed of yourself! If [900] wants you to go to the osteopath, you should go!"

A-4. She should go—just as has been directed in those elements and those conditions, that the greater experience may come in that way and manner. Again the lesson to the entity, and the verifications of the truths as are seen and have been given from time to time.

Q-11. Mother . . . and her home in Indiana. There seemed to be ghosts there.

A-11. Rather that indication of those fears, those thoughts that do enter in regarding the physical health of individuals of this household. Ghosts, then, of the mind, see? fear.

Q-12. My mother appeared to me. She said to me: "I am alive."

A-12. [Interrupting] She *is* alive!

Q-13. [Continuing] "Something is wrong with your sister's leg, or shoulder." (Or both—I don't clearly remember.) "She ought [to] see a doctor about it."

A-13. This, as is seen, to the entity, is that experience drawing closer and closer to that at-oneness with the spiritual forces manifest through the at-onement of the forces manifested in this material plane. For, as is seen, the mother, *through* the entity's *own* mind, is as the mother to all in that household. Warning, then, of conditions that may arise, and of conditions existent. Then, warn the sister as regarding same, see?   136-45

To provide a warning. We have already seen the potential warning function of a precognitive dream. In some instances such dream warnings are transmitted by departed souls who are still concerned about our well being. This is clearly depicted in the following case.

Q-1. Saw my mother [139]. She told me that I should warn my Aunt Helen against an accident. Helen seemed to get into an accident, get badly hurt, and my mother took sick from it.

A-1. This, as is presented, is an accident regarding getting injured in an automobile and street car accident. Be warned, then, and warn the body as regarding same, see? and when the body keeps in that way of being warned, or keeps from the car, then this may not be expected to happen, for here we have, as it were, the direct communication of the entity in the spirit plane with the entity in the material plane, the attunement being reached when the entity in the body-conscious mind being subjugated and an at-onement with the universal forces. This also shows the entity how that the entity in the spirit plane, or spirit entity, is mindful of conditions which transpire, exist, in the material plane, see? **136-48**

To depict borderland experiences of the deceased. We should not assume that people who have died suddenly have no problems or concerns in the borderland. Although the continuity of life—i.e., survival—is a certainty, there are still difficulties to be overcome. We may have dreams of a deceased loved one that show that person troubled or confused. This is a call to prayer for us. The prayer should be for that departed soul and for any earthly conditions that may be causing the soul to be troubled. Remember, "the spirit entity is mindful of conditions which transpire, exist, in the material plane." (136-48) It may well be that there are things going on here in material life, especially among family members, which have an upsetting effect upon the soul who has passed on.

Dreams of Dying

One of the potentially most disturbing dreams is the one in which death takes place. This can be the death of oneself or of another dream character. The recurrent theme in readings given on such dreams is: in order for something new to be born, something old must die.

Most frequently the meaning of one's own death in a dream is the awakening of something new in the dreamer. Often this awakening is of a deeper understanding of the mind or spirit. That is, in order to come to a greater awareness of the inner life, one must let go of—or die to—a merely physical notion of one's being. If one is physically dying in a dream the most likely interpretation is that a limited, physical concept of oneself is in the process of dying so that something new can be born. There is the possiblity that a dream of one's death is a physical health warning, and the dreamer should check this if he is concerned. However, fear of actually dying is usually the inappropriate response to such a dream.

Q-1. Dreamed I died.
A-1. This is the manifestation of the birth of thought and mental development awakening in the individual, as mental forces and physical forces develop. This, then, is the awakening of the subconscious, as is manifested in death in physical forces, being the birth in the mental. **136-6**

Q-7. What is the meaning of the dreams I had Wednesday night, Jan. 8th, in which I saw myself dead and embalmed?

A-7. The period of awakening, of arousing self to the greater opportunities and abilities that are before them.   1688-6

Related to the experience of actually dying in a dream is the experience of finding oneself already dead. This second type of dream is probably more rare than the dream of dying. Instead of symbolically indicating the awakening of a new mental or spiritual self, a dream in which the dreamer is already dead probably constitutes a lesson. This is the case in such dreams interpreted by Cayce (e.g., 900-99 and 140-10). The lesson concerns a *direct experience* of the nature of the connection between the physical realm and the spiritual realm. Through such a dream one may learn "to be able to bridge the chasm." (140-10) Perhaps this means to subsequently live daily life with a greater sensitivity to the ever-present influences of the spiritual realm.

Finally, there are dreams in which one of the dream characters is dying, especially a friend or family member. In some instances Cayce interpreted such dreams to indicate that the dying person represented an aspect of the dreamer's own psychological makeup (e.g., 136-70). In such dreams we might well ask ourselves, "What part of myself could this dream character symbolize and do I recognize a change taking place in that part of me?"

In other instances Cayce interpreted dreams of the death of others to indicate a change about to take place in that other person's life (i.e., a form of telepathic dream). The change could conceivably be physical death, but more likely a change of attitude or an inner awakening.

In one example (139-7) a woman with a terminal brain tumor dreamed that she saw every member of her family and they were dead. Cayce suggested that there was the potential for each one of these family members to have an awakening. They could die to those conditions that were preventing them from seeing clearly the forces that were at work in the dreamer's terminal illness. Apparently the dreamer could help each member of her family to the birth of a new awareness if she would adopt the proper attitude toward her own illness.

Conscious Previews of the Borderland

The key word in this section is "conscious." Through many dreams we gain a glimpse of inner worlds much like those we will know after death. However, in such experiences we rarely realize that we are explorers of these inner realms. Because we do not recognize what has happened to us until we awaken and remember it was a dream, we usually fail to gain the experiences we might have.

It is analogous to being on a long driving trip and seeing a sign along the road as you are *leaving* a small town. The sign indicates that this was a place of great historic significance. You had paid only half attention to the sights as you went through. Even though you could later tell your friends you had once been in that famous town, you really did not experience the place as fully as you might have.

Of course in the analogy, the town is the dream state; and whereas it may be possible in waking life to turn the car around and go back, we are rarely able to go back to sleep and enter the same dream with the full awareness that we are dreaming.

This phenomenon of knowing you are dreaming while still in the dream has come to be called "lucid dreaming." It is not a term found in the readings, and yet its principles can be identified in that material. That we should become explorers of the inner worlds is clearly recommended in the readings.

> . . . much more is experienced in the planes other than mere flesh, see? Hence, prepare self for earthly, for the every sphere of development, while the entity has that ability to view these various phases from the various viewpoints.   137-43

In other words, while we still have a physical body and conscious mind it is to our advantage to consciously examine the other dimensions of consciousness. This may be due to the fact that in the physical dimension we have a clearer sense of will or choice. We can evaluate the quality of each dimension after we experience it and make decisions as to whether or not that is a plane of experience we want to nurture for ourselves. Once we die, we may move to one of the dimensions of experience and have less opportunity to discriminate and evaluate the opportunities and difficulties it provides for us.

The seeker will no doubt wonder, "What will I find at these inner levels of awareness, these mental states that resemble experiences after death?" Answers are found in some of the great religious traditions, especially in Tibetan Buddhism. In the *Tibetan Book of the Dead* there is a careful description of the states between earthly incarnations—the Bardo state. There is some evidence to indicate that these teachings were read not only to the person who was dying, but were also used by spiritual seekers long before death. The concepts of this book were employed most effectively to explore and to come to understand the Borderland and other planes of the spiritual realm.

The concept in the readings is that upon moving into the spiritual world we will meet that which we have worshipped. This holds true for dreams whether they are lucid ones or not. The readings say it this way: "For, to be absent from the body is to be present with that ye have worshipped as thy God." (2796-1) Being "absent from the body" does not necessarily mean an out-of-body experience but rather moving away from a physical awareness of life (as we do in sleep). And so, if we are to meet what we have worshipped as we venture within, it behooves us to do important work with our ideals and beliefs. A person who desires to experience a conscious exploration of the inner life—such as through lucid dreaming—is strongly encouraged to make special efforts to attune his conscious thoughts in waking life to the best he knows.

Before considering certain principles from the readings pertinent to lucid dreaming, it would be well to clarify "where" such experiences take place. For many years before the concept of lucid dreaming caught on with dream theorists, there was much interest in out-of-body experiences (OOBE). Psychical researchers, curiosity seekers and many others, glorified the OOBE as a relatively advanced state of conscious attainment.

However, in the past ten years there has been important research in consciousness which suggests the need to re-evaluate the meaning of the OOBE. That work includes Raymond Moody's studies, as well as careful research of the Cayce readings such as that done by G. Scott Sparrow in *Lucid Dreaming.*

The problem is one of appropriateness. There is little doubt but that out-of-body experiences can take place. Careful research has strongly suggested the notion that we do have a higher or more subtle energy body that can allow the mind to experience independent of the flesh body. However, the question is just this: where is the best "place" for this more sensitive body to experience? Is it in the material world, perhaps floating around the bedroom or traveling across town to see a friend? Probably it can do this and yet for what purpose? We already have a flesh body that permits us to have experiences in materiality.

That higher-energy body—call it the finer physical body, astral body or whatever—is also capable of experiencing the spiritual realm, the dimensions of awareness beyond materiality. If we must localize those dimensions, we do best to say they are within. And so the answer to the question of appropriateness should be clear. In most cases it is a waste of time to try to have out-of-body experiences in the classical sense of the term. Except for the fact that they may convince the practitioner that he will survive bodily death, they probably serve no significant purpose. In fact, if this higher-energy body is the one we will have upon death, then through the OOBE we are practicing being an earth-bound soul!

The appropriate thing is to use this higher body as a vehicle to move within. Interestingly, some experiences that seem to be OOBE are actually ones that take place within the various levels of one's own mind. In the following example—which resembles cases found by Raymond Moody—Cayce points out that the experience did not take place in California but within herself.

Q-19. *In 1934, during my last surgical operation when I was thought dead, I traveled out of the body to California, to realms of light. Where did I go really and what was the meaning and purpose of the experience?*

A-19. This was a coordination of experiences the body had seen in the experiences of others; correlated with the edges of more than one experience to which the body had been subjected or subjugated in other experiences. As to place—within self. As to conditions—the many experiences of the entity, both mental *and* spiritual, in the various realms of consciousness.

As to its worth within self—the awareness of the universality of consciousness as may be obtained in the one light, that is *all* light.   2067-3

The Principle of Lucid Dreaming

Another term we might use for lucid dreaming is conscious (or self-reflective) experiencing at the fourth dimension. Recall that the fourth dimension is that inner world of thoughts and ideas. The self-awareness quality of a lucid dream—i.e., knowing in the dream that one is dreaming—permits greater *understanding* of what is happening in the dream.

The word "understanding" is the key. Particularly as we retain self-reflective consciousness within a dream we can see and understand the spiritual origin of things that exist in the material world. For example, suppose that a man is experiencing mysterious digestive troubles in waking life. In a dream he might confront particular symbols and events that depict the origin of his physical problem. Particularly if he becomes lucid in that dream he may have the opportunity to respond optimally to the dream events and symbols, thereby obtaining the maximum understanding available to him. In the words of the readings, in the fourth dimension a condition is reached whereby physical objects (i.e., material conditions) are spiritually understood. (see 900-66, A-9)

Conversely, in fourth-dimensional experience we have the opportunity to perceive spiritual things in terms of a form or appearance. That is, things that are really nonmaterial take on a shape and appear to us much as the material world does. This is exactly what takes place in a dream. A very elusive thing like an emotion can appear concretely to us as a dream image: perhaps a character or an animal. The opportunity for us is understanding.

Our job is to enhance that potential for understanding. We do it through dream study and application. Developing lucidity in the dream state is simply another tool. The development of this type of self-reflective awareness can be seen as a movement from subjectivity to objectivity in the dream. Another way of saying it is that we can move from being reactive in the dream to a point where we harness the will and carefully select our responses.

Usually we merely react to what is going on about us in the dream. We are in what would be called a subjective state because we are subject or subservient to the dream events as they unfold. Certain emotions particularly accentuate this subjective state. The readings identify fear as a good example and suggest that with such an emotion removed the dreamer becomes much more likely to understand the transitory (i.e., dream-like) quality of the experience:

> . . . *with* fear, creates no resistance and becomes *subject* to the conditions as are happening, but *with* the fear cast out . . . there comes the knowledge that this is only as transitory in its activity . . .   900-209

In his book *Lucid Dreaming,* G. Scott Sparrow has described some of the techniques and approaches the dreamer can employ in order to develop lucidity. Often the onset of lucidity is accompanied by the emergence of a discriminatory faculty— the recognition of paradoxes in the dream which suggest that this is a dream world. For example, one man dreamed that he awoke in his bedroom and turned his flashlight on the clock. No matter how he pointed the flashlight it wouldn't illuminate the face of the clock. In this dream he realized that this was impossible in waking life and that he must be dreaming.

One way to develop this type of discriminatory or critical faculty is through a reverie kind of re-dreaming. In waking life you can take dreams in which you did not become lucid and re-live them in detail. Practice identifying the elements or points in the dream events that could have revealed to you that this was a dream.

However, the most potent aid to the emergence of self-reflective consciousness in dreams is meditation. One way in which we could define meditation is the practice of becoming objective instead of subjective. Whenever we let the mind wander in meditation we have once again become subject to our memory patterns and imaginings. Through an act of will we must then refocus the mind in an objective way on the mantra, or to use Cayce's term, the affirmation. (See Appendix A for more on meditation.) It should be little wonder that many people who meditate in the middle of the night report a change in the quality of the dreams which occur just after the meditation period. Furthermore, many report the occurrence of lucidity in those post-meditation dreams.

The Use and Value of Lucidity

In those instances in which we realize that we are dreaming while still in the dream, we have a rare opportunity. Infrequent as this kind of dream may be, the potential for growth in understanding should not be overlooked. A lucid dream is not merely a curious phenomenon. It is a significant step forward on the ladder of evolution in consciousness.

The great writer, philosopher and mystic Rudolph Steiner spoke of something akin to lucid dreaming as the next step in our consciousness development. In his book *Cosmic Memory* he refers to it as self-conscious image consciousness, meaning the capacity to perceive the images we have created (i.e., our thought forms, such as the images of our dreams) while at the same time retaining a self-conscious or self-reflective awareness.

There are remarkable parallels which we find among the sources already mentioned such as Steiner and Cayce, and other theorists such as Celia Green (*Lucid Dreams*), Ann Faraday (*Dream Power*) and Carlos Casteñada (*Tales of Power*). They agree that the lucid dream is a special adventure into the inner world. It can be understood as a preview of the after-death state.

Because of its great potential for deeper self-understanding, it is especially crucial that the dreamer react properly in these unusual dreams. Though there may be a strong temptation to do so, the dreamer should not attempt to manipulate the contents or events of the dream! Unfortunately, some writers have misleadingly suggested doing just that. And while it is possible to change the dream into most anything you want, desire patterns will rarely lead you to the profound understanding and experiences possible in a lucid dream.

Instead, we should work with altering our *responses* in the dream to the characters and events around us. With this new-found objectivity we can use the will to select the most loving, constructive reaction to what is going on. The principle in this case is that the events of the dream are to a large extent determined by the attitudes, emotions and understandings of the dreamer. Occasionally, the mere awakening itself of lucidity will cause the dream to change. This is shown in the following instances, one of the few lucid dreams ever brought to Cayce.

Q-1. Dreamed that I was exercising in Kansas City. Walking up and down beside train taking me from Los Angeles to Chicago. I realized that I had left my overcoat in station and started for it when thought came to me that train might start. As I stood there undecided, the train started rapidly and I started running for vestibule. I couldn't make headway (as is customary in dreams) and I seemed to say to myself, this is only a dream as I can't run. With that thought I was released and ran easily and caught the train. **195-51**

Several ideas have already been suggested concerning the value of developing lucidity in the dream state. Such experience can give the dreamer a deeper understanding of the nature of after-death consciousness. This in itself can be quite valuable because it becomes personal proof of the survival of bodily death.

However, there are other benefits. Sometimes through lucidity the dreamer can learn to interpret the dream while it is still going on. Many people have reported excellent interpretative insights in this way. Others have found that they can confront and heal some personal problem in a symbolic fashion. For example, by changing the recurrent, subjective reaction of fear in a dream, the dreamer may be able to face and befriend some troublesome aspect of his life. Finally, and probably most important, the lucid dream can lead to more lucid living while awake. The same process holds true: we have a tendency to merely react subjectively to events in daily life. We need to learn to become more objective and try to change our own response patterns before trying to change others. Lucid dreaming can be a valuable rehearsal for such lucid living.

If the possibilities of lucid dreaming sound exciting to you, the things to consider are *expectations* and *purpose*. First, do not assume that all your dreams should suddenly become lucid ones. There will continue to be great value in normal dreams and a necessity for them. For most of us, lucid dreams will only be rare occurrences. We must have faith that self-reflective consciousness in dreams will emerge when we are truly ready for it *and* when it will be helpful to us in our growth.

However, our purpose should not be simply to have lucid dreams (or any particular quality of dream, for that matter). We are encouraged to seek attunement to the divine within, trusting that whatever measure of experience is best will be given. There is a wisdom in the unconscious that we can learn to rely on, instead of trying to prematurely force open the bud of developing consciousness. Even knowing that meditations in the middle of the night may enhance the likelihood of a special dream, we must take special care to keep the purpose of such meditation oneness with God.

Closely related to purpose is the question of a guiding influence in such inner experiences. Whether or not we pursue an exploration of the inner life should be determined by the motivating force that directs us. In this closing passage from the readings, Cayce responds to an inquiry about whether or not to allow conscious fourth-dimensional experiences to take place.

Q-8. Should I allow this to happen, or fight against it?
A-8. Depends on whether you know what you want to do with it or not! This is where individuals not able to control are apt to allow other forces to control them. Read the description and understand what's taking place. If there is the desire that the spirit of truth, the Master, direct—then there may be gained an understanding of the relationships between spirit and matter. If there is the desire that the masterfulness of self be experienced, or a domination for self—as experienced over not only the lower kingdom but of the higher kingdom as well—or if there is the desire for self-indulgence, or for mental exploration into the unknown, you'll find it—but it may make self unknown to the better interests of self. Hence it must be used properly, correctly. Pray about it. 1523-15

If we intend to use these special experiences merely to satisfy our curiosity or self-indulgent tendencies, it is better to leave them alone. Manipulating the content of dreams to fit desires is counterproductive. The same can be said of continually using such a state simply to fly or perform other feats not possible in materiality. However, the possibilities are tremendous—even to contact the Light itself—if we respond properly: adopt an attitude of love in the dream, surround self with the protective influence of the Ideal, try to be of service or to help others in the dream, and perhaps even turn to an affirmation and have a period of meditation in the dream.

Summary

In recent years there have been many new understandings of death and dying. More and more people recognize the certainity of the soul's survival of bodily death. A few individuals have come to this awareness through a near death experience in which they have apparently previewed the Borderland state. Others have had profound inner experiences that have convinced them of the continuity of life.

However, experiential proof of survival is available to all through dreams. Although we rarely take time to realize it, each night we rehearse the process of dying. In dreams we venture into non-material realms that approximate the after-death state. What is generally missing in ordinary dreams is any kind of self-awareness to help us realize that we are experiencing the reality of non-material life. With proper expectations and purposes the development of lucidity in the dream state can sharpen our understanding. We can see that death in the physical world will merely be a birth into another dimension of living.

The same principle holds true for dreams of death and dying. Although such dreams may occasionally be recognition of impending physical death, much more frequently a dream involving death represents the birth of a new awareness. When we find a dream character is dying, the following interpretative question can be helpful: "What part of myself could this dream character symbolize, and do I recognize a change taking place in that part of me?"

Exercises in Application

Select a dream in which a character you know from waking life is dead or dying. List characteristics of this person which may conceivably represent aspects of yourself. Assume for the moment that some of those characteristics are in a transition period. Which characteristics would you like to see die so that something new can be born in their place? Write what the new characteristics might be. Be sure that they would be in keeping with your highest ideal.

Example:
Dream character dying: My sister
Characteristics
    energetic
    critical (. . . could die and be replaced by . . .) sensitive, generous
    moody (. . . could die and be replaced by . . .) joyful

Then work at applying the potential new characteristics in daily life. Watch your dreams, particularly for how the same character may begin to appear in a different way in your dreams.

Epilogue

Having nearly reached the conclusion of this book, there may be some degree of confusion in your mind because of the large number of dream interpretative techniques that have been suggested. You may wonder, "Which one should I do first?" or "What if more than one technique seems to work on a particular dream?"

In answering these valid questions, we must first be aware that the unconscious mind—from which our dreams come— is not merely a hidden version of the conscious mind. That is, it can operate from a different perspective of reasoning and meaning. For example, our conscious minds have considerable difficulty with paradoxes. However, for the unconscious mind multiple levels of meaning are much more natural. A single dream may have several interpretations, each with its own value for the dreamer.

And so, the initial solution to the problem is to go ahead and try many approaches on a single dream because you may get several valuable interpretations from it. However, keep in mind that you never really know if you have arrived at a significant mental interpretation until you apply it in daily life. For example, suppose that you apply the many interpretation skills of this book to one of your dreams and find that three of them produce meaningful insights. However, suppose two of the three seemed to be contradictory. It is only by taking some preliminary steps in application that you can begin to get feedback to judge your insights. That feedback may come from another dream or it may come from waking life experiences. Remember the injunction, "By their fruits you shall know them." That rule of thumb will be your greatest friend when you have to evaluate the accuracy of possible interpretations you have arrived at. If you have set an ideal of personal growth, service and spiritual development, then proper dream interpretations will show you fruits of a more fulfilled life.

While working with the techniques of this book, also remember that they are not necessarily independent of each other. That is, many of the approaches support or enhance each other. By combining several of the techniques you may be more effective in your dream study. For example, the theme technique can be very helpful as you use several of the other approaches.

And a final suggestion which may be useful to you as you work with the many possible interpretations of a single dream: work with the alternatives one at a time. Even though the unconscious mind is skillful at creating dream images which have multiple levels of meaning, in the waking state we tend to operate best in a more focused manner. If you arrive at three possible meanings for one dream, then take three distinct periods of time to work on applying those three possible interpretations.

Appendix A
HOW TO MEDITATE
AN APPROACH FROM THE EDGAR CAYCE
READINGS

1. *Set an ideal or purpose for meditation.* It is suggested that one set a spiritual ideal for life. It can be expressed as a word or a short phrase that describes the highest spirit of living that one would like to have guiding every aspect of life. Another way of thinking of the term ideal is motivation. What is the highest motivation that you can conceive of, the one you would like to have directing you all the time.

2. *Select a time and place for meditation.* Consistency can be an important factor. Most people become more effective meditators by keeping a regular time of day. Choose the best time of day for you by deciding when you are most likely to be able to be alert and still keep your mind on your ideal.

3. *Complete preparatory activities.* The exact nature of these procedures will depend on personal preference. Each meditator should experiment with some or all of these activities, finding those that help create an optimal mental and physical state for meditation.

Dietary changes	Head and neck exercise	Chanting
Physical exercise	Breathing exercise	Incense
Cleansing	Music	Prayer (especially recommended)

4. *Focus attention on an affirmation.* During the actual silence period of meditation what one focuses attention upon is particularly important. Use an affirmation which is a short statement (usually about one sentence) which expresses the spiritual ideal you chose in step #1.

Repeat the affirmation several times until you begin to get a sense of its meaning. Focus attention on the meaning or the spirit of the affirmation. Do not just repeat the words over and over again. Whenever you become distracted (e.g., outside noise, irrelevant thoughts) gently bring your mind back by saying the affirmation again. Return to a silent focus upon the feeling, spirit or meaning of the affirmation.

5. *Prayer for others.* A part of the purpose for meditation is to be a better channel or servant to humanity. We can begin that process by taking time at the end of the meditation period to have prayers for those for whom we have concern.

What *is* meditation? ... it is the attuning of the mental body and the physical body to its spiritual source ... it is the attuning of thy physical and mental attributes seeking to know the relationships to the Maker. *That* is true meditation.   281-41

Meditation, then, is prayer, but is prayer from *within* the *inner* self, and partakes not only of the physical inner man but the soul that is aroused by the spirit of man from within.
281-13

Appendix B
DREAM THEMES

Q-9. A few nights ago. Saw my father, and it seemed he was operated on for appendicitis. I wanted to see the healed-up wound, but he was taking a bath. "Always take a warm bath after an operation," he told me. When he got out of the tub I was able to see and examine the scar left from the operation.
900-296

Possible wording of theme: Someone is having something removed.

Cayce's interpretation suggests that this is a lesson to the dreamer that from time to time, as he grows in understanding, it becomes necessary to "remove certain ideas." That is, the unfoldment of consciousness requires letting go of or purging old concepts and ideas that are no longer the best way to see things.

Q-2. I dreamed of being at a party or dance and of meeting there a girl, whom I've met, a Miss ... and with her a boy I've heard her speak of as George. Later it seemed that she was crying, saying that George wouldn't dance with her and was acting curiously, and she wanted to go home. It seemed that I assisted her in some way. I don't remember whether I danced with her or took her home, one or the other.   341-12

Possible wording of theme: I am helping someone who is troubled.

Cayce's interpretation suggests that the theme of service is itself the lesson of the dream. There will come a sense of satisfaction through serving others. Here the reading picks up on the fact that the girl was only a casual acquaintance and recommends that this theme of service can be applied even in contact with persons whom the dreamer does not know well.

An aeroplane rose in the sky trying for height, and for height only. Aeroplane came to a sudden and disastrous stop. Starts its sudden crash for earth, leaving a wake of flame from fire. Plane seemed to be in vicinity of Mt. Washington, a high mountain in the White Mountain Range. Did not see plane land, but outstanding features were: 1. Height of plane. 2. Sudden stop and downward rush. 3. Wake of flame from burning plane. 137-10

Possible wording of dream: Something climbs too high, only to end up in destruction.

Cayce's interpretation relates this theme to the dreamer's desire for fame and notoriety, especially through development of the psychic forces. It then warns against such an attitude, which would only lead to detrimental conditions.

Dreamed of going to a pond with my brother. I saw a great many fish of all sizes swimming about in the water. The bottom of the pond was muddy but the water was clear. Several slimy animals started to crawl up the bank and we threw clods of dirt at them. On seeing a group of what I supposed to be hornets clustered on the side of the bank, I threw a clod at them and told my brother to run. We ran back to the house. There I met [419] and asked him to help me find some cord and hooks so that we might go back and catch some fish. 341-13

Possible wording of theme: Help is asked for in order to complete a search activity.

Cayce's interpretation points to the necessity of *having aid* in order "to be able to attain that desired in life's pathway." An alternative theme, related to "running away from something dangerous" (i.e., the hornets), apparently was not pertinent to the dreamer's waking life, or at least was not the most significant message of the dream.

Appendix C
SOME QUESTIONS AND ANSWERS

Q. What is the meaning of a recurrent dream and how can I make it stop?
A. A recurrent dream probably refers to some problem or difficulty in consciousness that is extremely important. It may be important from the perspective of the soul or it may have

gained importance by the conscious concern and worry you give to it while awake.

Use the techniques described in this book to discover the meaning of a recurrent dream, just as you would any other dream. However, realize that the dream will not stop simply because you intellectually figure out what it means. You should expect it to continue until you have changed or healed that within yourself to which the recurrent dream refers.

Q. What if a dream does not immediately seem to have an interpretation?

A. We may occasionally have a dream that is simply a rehash of the previous day's experience and which actually has no further meaning. Or we may have dreams which merely reflect physical stimuli and have no other interpretation. For example, there is the dream of being in the Arctic, only to awaken and find that you have left the window open and a cold breeze is blowing through the room.

However, we should not be too quick to write off our dreams as having no interpretation simply because we see no immediate solution. Many people have reported that it is only after several weeks that they begin to gain insight on some dreams. Sometimes the time period is even longer. With this in mind, we are probably best off to carefully record all of our dreams and keep looking back to those which we did not figure out the first time we tried.

We should also be careful about dismissing a dream as a rehash of the previous day's experiences. Many of our dreams will use the experiences of yesterday as a kind of dream vocabulary to get across some other message. Just because a character or situation from the previous day appears in the dream, it is safer to assume that he is reappearing in your dream for some distinct purpose.

Q. What does it mean if I have the same dream as someone else?

A. The meaning of the *process* of mutual dreaming is a demonstration of certain laws of the unconscious mind. It shows us that we are in fact one with each other at a deep level of the mind. Cayce's readings state that all subconscious minds are in contact with one another. Mutual dreaming may be an expression of this fact. However, we should keep in mind that every shared dream is not necessarily due to our connections at deep levels of mind. For example, we share many conscious experiences each day with people of our community (e.g., the daily weather, the daily news, etc.) and they may be reflected in similar dreams.

Q. What does the symbol _____ mean in my dream? (Fill in most any symbol you want in that blank space.)

A. This is an extremely difficult question to answer accurately for someone. Even if you make a lucky or intuitive guess, you may have misled the questioner into thinking that a dream can be treated in a fragmentary way. Usually we must know both the context in which the symbol was used in the dream, plus the personal associations that the dreamer might have with that object or person.

However, we occasionally have dream symbols that are of a universal or archetypal nature. A good resource to learn about those kinds of symbols is Carl Jung's writings on symbology (e.g., *Man and His Symbols*). For those who are interested in symbology from the perspective of the Cayce readings, they should check the comprehensive index of symbols at the end of *Dreams and Dreaming,* Volume 2 (available to members as a two-volume set from A.R.E. Press, Virginia Beach, Virginia 23451). This is a collection of all the dream readings of Edgar Cayce and the index allows the reader to check on how Cayce interpreted particular symbols.

Q. *What does it mean when I dream I am falling?*

A. This is a frequently reported theme in people's dreams. The first step would be to examine your daily life for evidence of that very theme. Are you in the process of falling in some way during waking life experiences? There are various ways in which we can fall: prestige, power, finances, etc. Or it may be that we are not yet falling in some way but fear that this could soon happen to us. In such cases the dream is merely giving us the chance to face or become more aware of our emotions and attitudes in this regard.

Another possible meaning of a dream of falling relates to what happens as we go to sleep. There is a separation that takes place as the awareness of the mind leaves the material, physical plane. It is interesting to note that the various phrases we use for going to sleep suggest that this is appropriate imagery for the process: "falling asleep" and "dropping off to sleep." In other words, the experience is so commonplace that it has even crept into our language. Rather than be frightened by such experiences, we should have the sense that this is a frequent way in which the mind expresses the fact that it is making a shift in consciousness.

Q. *Can we dream of our past lives?*

A. Certainly reincarnation is only a theory. Although there is evidence for it, we cannot say that it has been proven. The approaches to dream study outlined in this book do not require a belief either way on the question of reincarnation. However, a willingness to look at the possibility that you have been in the earth before (in *human* form) may help you understand a certain quality of dream that may come occasionally. When we dream of being in situations that resemble historic conditions (i.e., before our birth) we may be gaining insights of previous incarnations. However, an equally plausible interpretation would be that we desire to be identified with those times; or, we have read about those times and the dream merely incorporates those scenes into the action.

No matter what you decide about the question of past life recall through dreams, be sure to look more deeply into these particular dream experiences. Most likely a past life dream would not come simply to entertain you. It would come because it helps you understand a daily life problem or to answer a question that has troubled you. Discovering that meaning should be the focus of your work with the dream, rather than worrying about its historic authenticity.

Q. How should one work with the dreams that children have?

A. The most important thing to do with children and their dreams is to listen. Especially before the teenage years it is not necessary to teach a child the intellectual tools of dream interpretation. What is important is that the child would develop a sense of being comfortable with the inner world of dreams. Knowing that a parent is always ready to listen to a dream can be very valuable. Many families have found that breakfast table discussions of the previous night's dream is particularly worth while.

About the author:

Mark Thurston, Ph.D., is Director of the Educational Division of the Association of Research and Enlightenment, Inc. He received his B.A. from the University of Texas and his M.A. in psychology from West Georgia College. His Ph.D. is from the Humanistic Psychology Institute. He is the author of *Experiments in a Search for God, Experiments in Practical Spirituality, Understand and Develop Your ESP, Discovering Your Soul's Purpose, How to Change Your Attitudes and Emotions,* and co-author of *Meditation and the Mind of Man.*

DISCOVER HOW THE EDGAR CAYCE MATERIAL CAN HELP YOU!

The Association for Research and Enlightenment, Inc. (A.R.E.®), was founded in 1931 by Edgar Cayce. Its international headquarters are in Virginia Beach, Virginia, where thousands of visitors come year round. Many more are helped and inspired by A.R.E.'s local activities in their own hometowns or by contact via mail (and now the Internet!) with A.R.E. headquarters.

People from all walks of life, all around the world, have discovered meaningful and life-transforming insights in the A.R.E. programs and materials, which focus on such areas as holistic health, dreams, family life, finding your best vocation, reincarnation, ESP, meditation, personal spirituality, and soul growth in small-group settings. Call us today on our toll-free number

1-800-333-4499

or

Explore our electronic visitor's center on the
INTERNET: http://www.are-cayce.com

We'll be happy to tell you more about how the work of the A.R.E. can help you!

A.R.E.
67th Street and Atlantic Avenue
P.O. Box 595
Virginia Beach, VA 23451-0595